"And say: Truth has come and falsehood has vanished away. Lo! falsehood is ever bound to vanish."
(17:81)

THE DOCTRINE OF AHL AL-SUNNA VERSUS THE "SALAFI" MOVEMENT

by Jamal Effendi al-`Iraqi al-Sidqi al-Zahawi
(d. 1936)

A COMPLETE REFUTATION
TRANSLATED INTO ENGLISH
WITH INTRODUCTION AND NOTES

Shaykh Muhammad Hisham Kabbani

As-Sunna Foundation of America
1996

Shaykh Muhammad Hisham Kabbani,
c/o As-Sunna Foundation of America
607A W. Dana St.
Mountain View, CA 94041
Email: asfa@world.com

Distributed by:
KAZI Publications, Inc.
3023 W. Belmont
Chicago, IL 60618
Tel: 312-267-7001; FAX: 312-267-7002

Edited by Gabriel F. Haddad, Ph.D. (Columbia)
Abdul Ghani Paul Hardy, Ph.D. (Chicago)

Library of Congress Cataloging in Publication Data

Al-Zahawi, Jamil Effendi Sidqi (1863-1936)
[al-fajr al-sadiq fi al-radd `ala munkiri al-tawassul wa al-khawariq. English]
The Doctrine of Ahl al-Sunna Versus the "Salafi" Movement / translated by Shaykh Muhammad Hisham Kabbani.
p.120 cm.
Indices.
1. Islam--doctrines. 2. Heretics, Muslim. 3. Islamic sects. 4. Wahhabiyah. I. Kabbani, Shaykh Muhammad Hisham. II. Title.

ISBN: 1-871031-47-8

CONTENTS

CONTENTS

THE DOCTRINE OF AHL AL-SUNNA VERSUS THE "SALAFI" MOVEMENT

بســـم ا لله الرحمن الرحيـــم

وصلى ا لله على سيدنا محمـد وآلـه وصحبه وسلّم

"And say: Truth has come and falsehood has vanished away. Lo! falsehood is ever bound to vanish."
(17:81)

Praise belongs to God Who has made truth clearly distinct from error, who puts down innovation and innovators and raises high the Sunna of the Prophet, Peace be upon him, and the people who follow it. Praise belongs to God Who in every century inspires a group of scholarly people to defend the Way of the Prophet, Peace be upon him, from the distortions of the ignorant -- those who call the majority of Muslims *mushrik* (idolaters) and *mubtadi`* (innovators) and *kafir* (disbelievers), falsely claiming that they alone are saved. Salutations and greetings upon the Prophet, his Family, and his Companions who are the exemplars and guardians of the Sunna.

The reason for this book This brief but excellent book by the Iraqi scholar al-Zahawi (1863-1936) is published in English for the first time, by Allah's grace, to give our Muslim brother in the West the necessary historical background on important questions of belief and methodology which are currently under attack from certain quarters of our Community. It is a companion volume to our two books entitled *Islamic Doctrine and Beliefs According to Ahl al-Sunna.*[1]

Islam, in our understanding and that of the majority of Muslims, both scholars and non-scholars, is the Islam of Ahl al-Sunna wa al-Jama`a -- The People of the Way of the Prophet and the Community of Muslims. Chief and foremost among them are the true Salaf of Islam: the Companions, the Successors, and their Successors according to the Prophet's sound hadith in Muslim: "The best century is my century, then the one following it, then the one following that." All the scholars understood by that hadith that the true Salaf were the models of human behavior and correct belief for us Muslims and for all mankind, that to follow them was to follow the Prophet, and that to follow the Prophet was to achieve salvation according to God's order: "Whoever obeys the Prophet obeys God" (4:80).

In our time, however, the name Salaf has been usurped by a movement which seeks to impose its own narrow interpretation of Religion towards a re-fashioning of the teachings of Islam. The adherents of this movement call themselves "Salafi." Such an appellation is baseless since the true Salaf knew no such school as the "Salafi" school nor even called themselves by that name; the only general name they recognized for themselves was that of Muslim. As an eminent scholar has stated, the Salafiyya is not a recognized school of thought in Islam, rather, it refers to a blessed historical period of our glorious past.

In reality, today's so-called "Salafi" movement, now about thirty years old, is the modern outgrowth of an two-century old

---

[1]Vol. I and II, pub. As-Sunnah Foundation of America (1996).

heresy spawned by a scholar of the Najd area in the Eastern part of the Arabian peninsula by the name of Muhammad ibn `Abd al-Wahhab (1703-1792). This scholar has been refuted by a long line of scholars both in his time and ours. Their names and the titles of some of their excellent refutations are found in the bibliography given at the end of this introduction.

In essence, Salafism and Wahhabism are the same, but the latter is identified by its founder while the former takes the name of the Salaf and makes it its own. Yet both Salafism and Wahhabism depart from the belief and practice of the Salaf, as the present book abundantly makes clear.

About the book Al-Zahawi displays a profound mastery of the proofs of Ahl al-Sunna which he presents in a clear and systematic style. The book is divided into concise sections tracing the origins of the Wahhabi/Salafi movement and the teachings that this movement promotes in isolation of the doctrine of the majority of Muslims. After a brief historical overview of the bloody origins of Wahhabism and the "Salafi" creed, the author turns to investigate the foundations of the shari`a which have been targeted by the Wahhabi/Salafi movement for revision, namely:

- the Wahhabi/Salafi tampering of the doctrine of the pious Salaf concerning God's essence and attributes, and his freedom from body, size, or direction;
- their rejection of *ijma`* (scholarly consensus) and *qiyas* (analogy);
- their rejection of the sources and methodological foundations of *ijtihad* (deriving qualified judgment) and *taqlid* (following qualified judgment).

The author then narrows down on the Wahhabi/Salafi practice of takfir, which is their declaring Muslims unbelievers, according to criteria not followed by the pious Salaf but devised by modern-day "Salafis." The author shows that the "Salafis" went out of bounds in condemning the Umma (Muslim Community) on the question of taqlid, declaring unbelievers all those who practice taqlid, that is, the majority of Muslims. Finally, the author turns to the linchpin of "Salafi" philosophy: leaving the ijma` of the true Salaf in declaring unbelievers all Muslims who use the Prophet Muhammad's intercession, Peace be upon him, as a *wasila* or means of blessing.

About the author Al-Shaykh Jamil Effendi al-Siqdi al-Zahawi was the son of the Mufti of Iraq and a descendant of Khalid ibn al-Walid. He was educated in the Islamic sciences chiefly by his father and, besides going on to become the greatest Arabic and Persian poet of modern Iraq, was also a literary master in the other two Islamic languages of the time: Turkish and Kurdish.

Al-Zahawi gave early proofs of his scholarly talents. By the age of forty he had served on the board of education in Baghdad, as the director of the state printing office, as editor of the chief state publication, *al-Zawra'*, and as a member of the Baghdad court of appeal. The second half of his life was devoted to writing, journalism, and teaching. He taught philosophy and Arabic literature in Istanbul and law in Baghdad. A prolific writer, at one point he declined the office of court poet and historian of Iraq offered him by King Faysal. In addition to the above he was scientifically inclined and wrote papers on various scientific topics such as electricity and the power of repulsion, all this despite a chronic disease of the spine which had crippled him from his twenty-fifth year.

At the turn of the century Arabia had witnessed the return of the Wahhabis to power and the open rebellion of their forces against the Caliph of the Islamic community. What was worse, the Wahhabi heresy was knocking at the gates of Baghdad, and the scholars of Ahl al-Sunna spoke out in order to stem its rising tide. In 1905 at the age of 42 and upon the request of his father al-Zahawi published this eloquent indictment of the sect's innovations in doctrine and jurisprudence, refuting its tenets one by one. He named the book, of which the present work forms the major part,

al-Fajr al-sadiq fi al-radd `ala munkiri al-tawassul wa al-khawariq ("The True Dawn: A Refutation of Those Who Deny The Validity of Using Means to God and the Miracles of Saints"). The title indicates Zahawi's opinion, reminiscent of that of other scholars who wrote similar refutations, that the Wahhabi position on tawassul represents the essence of their deviation from the beliefs of Ahl al-Sunna, although it is but one of their many divergences with Sunni Muslims.

Zahawi's brilliant style, his acute sense of balance and moderation, and his luminous logic and concision gave this brief book an undisputed place of honor among modern works of heresiology. May Allah reward him with His generosity, as well as those who collaborated on this timely and all-beneficial translation for the edification of English-speaking Muslims. We warmly recommend this book to all the sincere students and teachers who are interested in the growth and dissemination of sound Islamic belief in the West. As Sayyidina `Umar said, "This Religion is our flesh and our blood, so watch from whom you take it": in our time it is a duty to inform ourselves as to the soundness of the religious teaching which we are receiving and passing on to our children. For our own sake and theirs, we must discern the sources of such teaching with extreme caution, sifting the sound from the unsound, correcting what is wrong with our hand, our tongue, and our heart.

Muslims of the twenty-first century should beware of the renewed onslaught on their beliefs being conducted today from within our Communities East and West. In the name of Qur'an and Sunna, but actually supported by certain regimes pursuing specific ideologies, "Salafis" are taking over the mosques built by Ahl al-Sunna in Europe and North America -- mostly Indian and Pakistani immigrants -- by means of elections and fundings. It is the duty of all Muslims to ascertain that the mosques of Allah continue as centers of sound Islamic practice, not "Salafi" practice. This can only be done if one first appraises oneself of the reality of "Salafi" beliefs which are different from those of the main body of Muslims.

The Prophet said, Peace be upon him: "My Community will split into seventy-three sects. All of them will be in the fire except one group." They asked: "Who are they, O Messenger of Allah?" He said: "Those that follow my way and that of my companions."[2] This is a rallying-cry to the Firm Rope of 1,417 years of mainstream Islam and an invitation to reject the absurd claim of the "Salafi" movement that it is they, and not Ahl al-Sunna, who are the Saved Group. As Zahawi asks -- may Allah have mercy on him: If the saved group are those who came after Muhammad ibn `Abd al-Wahhab, then what is the status of all those who came before him, and that of the majority of those who came after him -- that is, Ahl al-Sunna wa al-Jama`a?

This warning is not meant as an attack on Islamic unity. On the contrary, our cry of alarm must be understood as a reaffirmation that the Saved Group which the Prophet mentioned in his hadith are the People of the Way of the Prophet and their scholars. Those scholars have spoken in no uncertain terms in condemnation of the innovations of Wahhabis and "Salafis" in our time, as the present book and the bibliography below, al-hamdu lillah, prove beyond doubt.

May Allah give victory to those who stand truly for the way of His Prophet, Blessings and Peace be upon him. O Believers, read this book and take heed of its message. We conclude this brief introduction with a selective list of authors and works of Ahl al-Sunna scholars in whose pages the deviations of Wahhabis and Salafis are exposed time after time and conclusively refuted. We look forward to their translations and recommend every one of them. And all praise belongs to God, the Lord of the Worlds.

Shaykh Hisham Muhammad Kabbani
Los Altos, California
1 Muharram 1417
19 May 1996

---

[2] A sound (sahih) hadith related by Tirmidhi, Abu Dawud, and al-Darimi.

AHL AL-SUNNA CONDEMNATIONS OF THE WAHHABI/SALAFI HERESIES: A SELECT BIBLIOGRAPHY

Al-Ahsa'i Al-Misri, Ahmad (1753-1826): Unpublished manuscript of a refutation of the Wahhabi sect. His son Shaykh Muhammad ibn Ahmad ibn `Abd al-Latif al-Ahsa'i also wrote a book refuting them.

Al-Ahsa'i, Al-Sayyid `Abd al-Rahman: wrote a sixty-seven verse poem which begins with the verse:
Badat fitnatun kal layli qad ghattatil aafaaqa
wa sha``at fa kadat tublighul gharba wash sharaqa
[A confusion came about like nightfall covering the skies
and became widespread almost reaching the whole world]

**Al-`Amrawi**, `Abd al-Hayy, and `Abd al-Hakim Murad (Qarawiyyin University, Morocco): *Al-tahdhir min al-ightirar bi ma ja'a fi kitab al-hiwar* ["Warning Against Being Fooled By the Contents of the Book (by Ibn Mani`) *A Debate With al-Maliki* (an attack on Ibn `Alawi al-Maliki by a Wahhabi writer)"] (Fes: Qarawiyyin, 1984).

**`Ata' Allah** al-Makki: *al-sarim al-hindi fil `unuq al-najdi* ["The Indian Scimitar on the Najdi's Neck"].

Al-Azhari, `Abd Rabbih ibn Sulayman al-Shafi`i (The author of *Sharh Jami' al-Usul li ahadith al-Rasul*, a basic book of Usul al-Fiqh: *Fayd al-Wahhab fi Bayan Ahl al-Haqq wa man dalla `an al-*

sawab, 4 vols. ["Allah's Outpouring in Differentiating the True Muslims From Those Who Deviated From the Truth"].

**Al-`Azzami**, `Allama al-shaykh Salama (d. 1379H): *Al-Barahin al-sati`at* ["The Radiant Proofs..."].

Al-Barakat al-Shafi`i al-Ahmadi al-Makki, `Abd al-Wahhab ibn Ahmad: unpublished manuscript of a refutation of the Wahhabi sect.

al-Bulaqi, Mustafa al-Masri wrote a refutation to San`a'i's poem in which the latter had praised Ibn `Abd al-Wahhab. It is in Samnudi's "Sa`adat al-Darayn" and consists in 126 verses beginning thus:
Bi hamdi wali al-hamdi la al-dhammi astabdi
Wa bil haqqi la bil khalqi lil haqqi astahdi
[By the glory of the Owner of glory, not baseness, do I overcome;
And by Allah, not by creatures, do I seek guidance to Allah]

Al-Buti, Dr. Muhammad Sa`id Ramadan (University of Damascus): *Al-salafiyyatu marhalatun zamaniyyatun mubarakatun la madhhabun islami* ["The Salafiyya is a blessed historical period not an Islamic school of law"] (Damascus: Dar al-fikr, 1988); *Al-lamadhhabiyya akhtaru bid`atin tuhaddidu al-shari`a al-islamiyya* ["Non-madhhabism is the most dangerous innovation presently menacing Islamic law"] (Damascus: Maktabat al-Farabi, n.d.).

Al-Dahesh ibn `Abd Allah, Dr. (Arab University of Morocco), ed. *Munazara `ilmiyya bayna `Ali ibn Muhammad al-Sharif wa al-Imam Ahmad ibn Idris fi al-radd `ala Wahhabiyyat Najd, Tihama, wa `Asir* ["Scholarly Debate Between the Sharif and Ahmad ibn Idris Against the Wahhabis of Najd, Tihama, and `Asir"].

Dahlan, al-Sayyid Ahmad ibn Zayni (d. 1304/1886). Mufti of Mecca and Shaykh al-Islam (highest religious authority in the Ottoman jurisdiction) for the Hijaz region: *al-Durar al-saniyyah fi al-radd ala al-Wahhabiyyah* ["The Pure Pearls in Answering the

Wahhabis"] pub. Egypt 1319 & 1347 H; *Fitnat al-Wahhabiyyah* ["The Wahhabi Fitna"]; *Khulasat al-Kalam fi bayan Umara' al-Balad al-Haram* ["The Summation Concerning the Leaders of the Sacrosanct Country"], a history of the Wahhabi fitna in Najd and the Hijaz.

al-Dajwi, Hamd Allah: *al-Basa'ir li Munkiri al-tawassul ka amthal Muhd. Ibn `Abdul Wahhab* ["The Evident Proofs Against Those Who Deny the Seeking of Intercession Like Muhammad Ibn `Abdul Wahhab"].

Shaykh al-Islam **Dawud ibn Sulayman** al-Baghdadi al-Hanafi (1815-1881 CE): *al-Minha al-Wahbiyya fi radd al-Wahhabiyya* ["The Divine Dispensation Concerning the Wahhabi Deviation"]; *Ashadd al-Jihad fi Ibtal Da`wa al-Ijtihad* ["The Most Violent Jihad in Proving False Those Who Falsely Claim Ijtihad"].

Al-Falani al-Maghribi, al-Muhaddith Salih: authored a large volume collating the answers of scholars of the Four Schools to Muhammad ibn `Abd al-Wahhab.

al-Habibi, Muhammad `Ashiq al-Rahman: *`Adhab Allah al-Mujdi li Junun al-Munkir al-Najdi* ["Allah's Terrible Punishment for the Mad Rejector From Najd"].

Al-Haddad, al-Sayyid al-`Alawi ibn Ahmad ibn Hasan ibn al-Qutb Sayyidi `Abd Allah ibn `Alawi al-Haddad al-Shafi`i: *al-Sayf al-batir li `unq al-munkir `ala al-akabir* ["The Sharp Sword for the Neck of the Assailant of Great Scholars"]. Unpublished manuscript of about 100 folios; *Misbah al-anam wa jala' al-zalam fi radd shubah al-bid`i al-najdi al-lati adalla biha al-`awamm* ["The Lamp of Mankind and the Illumination of Darkness Concerning the Refutation of the Errors of the Innovator From Najd by Which He Had Misled the Common People"]. Published 1325H.

Al-Hamami al-Misri, Shaykh Mustafa: *Ghawth al-`ibad bi bayan al-rashad* ["The Helper of God's Servants According to the Affirmation of Guidance"].

Al-Hilmi al-Qadiri al-Iskandari, Shaykh Ibrahim: **Jalal al-haqq fi kashf ahwal ashrar al-khalq** ["The Splendor of Truth in Exposing the Worst of People] (pub. 1355H).

Al-Husayni, `Amili, Muhsin (1865-1952). *Kashf al-irtiyab fi atba` Muhammad ibn `Abd al-Wahhab* ["The Dispelling of Doubt Concerning the Followers of Muhammad ibn `Abd al-Wahhab"]. [Yemen?]: Maktabat al-Yaman al-Kubra, 198?.

**Ibn `Abd al-Latif** al-Shafi`i, `Abd Allah: *Tajrid sayf al-jihad `ala mudda`i al-ijtihad* ["The drawing of the sword of jihad against the false claimants to ijtihad"].

The family of **Ibn `Abd al-Razzaq** al-Hanbali in Zubara and Bahrayn possess both manuscript and printed refutations by scholars of the Four Schools from Mecca, Madina, al-Ahsa', al-Basra, Baghdad, Aleppo, Yemen and other Islamic regions.

**Ibn `Abd al-Wahhab** al-Najdi, `Allama al-Shaykh Sulayman, elder brother of Muhammad ibn `Abd al-Wahhab: *al-Sawa'iq al-Ilahiyya fi al-radd 'ala al-Wahhabiyya* ["Divine Lightnings in Answering the Wahhabis"]. Ed. Ibrahim Muhammad al-Batawi. Cairo: Dar al-insan, 1987. Offset reprint by Waqf Ikhlas, Istanbul: Hakikat Kitabevi, 1994. Prefaces by Shaykh Muhammad ibn Sulayman al-Kurdi al-Shafi`i and Shaykh Muhammad Hayyan al-Sindi (Muhammad Ibn `Abd al-Wahhab's shaykh) to the effect that Ibn `Abd al-Wahhab is "dall mudill" ("misguided and misguiding").

**Ibn `Abidin** al-Hanafi, al-Sayyid Muhammad Amin: *Radd al-muhtar `ala al-durr al-mukhtar*, Vol. 3, Kitab al-Iman, Bab al-bughat ["Answer to the Perplexed: A Commentary on "The Chosen Pearl,"" Book of Belief, Chapter on Rebels]. Cairo: Dar al-Tiba`a al-Misriyya, 1272 H.

**Ibn `Afaliq** al-Hanbali, Muhammad Ibn `Abdul Rahman: *Tahakkum al-muqallidin bi man idda`a tajdid al-din* [Sarcasm of the muqallids against the false claimants to the Renewal of Religion]. A very comprehensive book refuting the Wahhabi heresy and posting questions which Ibn `Abdul Wahhab and his followers were unable to answer for the most part.

Ibn Dawud al-Hanbali, `Afif al-Din `Abd Allah: *as-sawa`iq wa al-ru`ud* ["Lightnings and thunder"], a very important book in 20 chapters. According to the Mufti of Yemen Shaykh al-`Alawi ibn Ahmad al-Haddad, the mufti of Yemen, "This book has received the approval of the `ulama of Basra, Baghdad, Aleppo, and Ahsa' [Arabian peninsula]. It was summarized by Muhammad ibn Bashir the qadi of Ra's al-Khayma in Oman."

Ibn Ghalbun al-Libi also wrote a refutation in forty verses of al-San`ani's poem in which the latter had praised Ibn `Abd al-Wahhab. It is in Samnudi's *Sa`adat al-darayn* and begins thus:
Salami `ala ahlil isabati wal-rushdi
Wa laysa `ala najdi wa man halla fi najdi
[My salutation is upon the people of truth and guidance
And not upon Najd nor the one who settled in Najd]

Ibn Khalifa `Ulyawi al-Azhari: *Hadhihi `aqidatu al-salaf wa al-khalaf fi dhat Allahi ta`ala wa sifatihi wa af`alihi wa al-jawab al-sahih li ma waqa`a fihi al-khilaf min al-furu` bayna al-da`in li al-salafiyya wa atba` al-madhahib al-arba`a al-islamiyya* ["This is the doctrine of the Predecessors and the Descendants concerning the divergences in the branches between those who call to *al-salafiyya* and the followers of the Four Islamic Schools of Law"] (Damascus: Matba`at Zayd ibn Thabit, 1398/1977.

Kawthari al-Hanafi, Muhammad Zahid. *Maqalat al-Kawthari*. (Cairo: al-Maktabah al-Azhariyah li al-Turath, 1994).

Al-Kawwash al-Tunisi, `Allama Al-Shaykh Salih: his refutation of the Wahhabi sect is contained in Samnudi's volume: "Sa`adat al-darayn fi al-radd `ala al-firqatayn."

Khazbek, Shaykh Hasan: *Al-maqalat al-wafiyyat fi al-radd `ala al-wahhabiyyah* ["Complete Treatise in Refuting the Wahhabis"].

Makhluf, Muhammad Hasanayn: *Risalat fi hukm al-tawassul bil-anbiya wal-awliya* ["Treatise on the Ruling Concerning the Use of Prophets and Saints as Intermediaries"].

Al-Maliki al-Husayni, Al-muhaddith Muhammad al-Hasan ibn `Alawi: *Mafahimu yajibu an tusahhah* ["Notions that should be corrected"] 4th ed. (Dubai: Hashr ibn Muhammad Dalmuk, 1986); *Muhammad al-insanu al-kamil* ["Muhammad, the Perfect Human Being"] 3rd ed. (Jeddah: Dar al-Shuruq, 1404/1984).

Al-Mashrifi al-Maliki al-Jaza'iri: *Izhar al-`uquq mimman mana`a al-tawassul bil nabi wa al-wali al-saduq* ["The Exposure of the Disobedience of Those Who Forbid Using the Intermediary of the Prophets and the Truthful Saints].

Al-Mirghani al-Ta'ifi, `Allama `Abd Allah ibn Ibrahim (d. 1793): *Tahrid al-aghbiya' `ala al-Istighatha bil-anbiya' wal-awliya* ["The Provocations of the Ignorant Against Seeking the Help of Prophets and Saints"] (Cairo: al-Halabi, 1939).

Mu'in al-Haqq al-Dehlawi (d. 1289): *Sayf al-Jabbar al-maslul `ala a`da' al-Abrar* ["The Sword of the Almighty Drawn Against the Enemies of the Pure Ones"].

Al-Muwaysi al-Yamani, `Abd Allah ibn `Isa: Unpublished manuscript of a refutation of the Wahhabi sect.

Al-Nabahani al-Shafi`i, al-qadi al-muhaddith Yusuf ibn Isma`il (1850-1932): *Shawahid al-Haqq fi al-istighatha bi sayyid al-Khalq (s)* ["The Proofs of Truth in the Seeking of the Intercession of the Prophet"].

Al-Qabbani al-Basri al-Shafi`i, Allama Ahmad ibn `Ali: A manuscript treatise in approximately 10 chapters.

Al-Qadumi al-Nabulusi al-Hanbali: `AbdAllah: *Rihlat* ["Journey"].

Al-Qazwini, Muhammad Hasan, (d. 1825). *Al-Barahin al-jaliyyah fi raf` tashkikat al-Wahhabiyah* ["The Plain Demonstrations That Dispel the Aspersions of the Wahhabis"]. Ed. Muhammad Munir al-Husayni al-Milani. 1st ed. Beirut: Mu'assasat al-Wafa', 1987.

Al-Qudsi: *al-Suyuf al-Siqal fi A`naq man ankara `ala al-awliya ba`d al-intiqal* ["The Burnished Swords on the Necks of Those Who Deny the Role of Saints After Their Leaving This World"].

**Al-Rifa`i**, Yusuf al-Sayyid Hashim, President of the World Union of Islamic Propagation and Information: *Adillat Ahl al-Sunna wa al-Jama`at aw al-radd al-muhkam al-mani` `ala munkarat wa shubuhat Ibn Mani` fi tahajjumihi `ala al-sayyid Muhammad `Alawi al-Maliki al-Makki* ["The Proofs of the People of the Way of the Prophet and the Muslim Community: or, the Strong and Decisive Refutation of Ibn Mani`'s Aberrations and Aspersions in his Assault on Muhammad `Alawi al-Maliki al-Makki"] (Kuwait: Dar al-siyasa, 1984).

Al-Samnudi al-Mansuri, al-`Allama al-Shaykh Ibrahim: *Sa`adat al-darayn fi al-radd `ala al-firqatayn al-wahhabiyya wa muqallidat al-zahiriyyah* ["Bliss in the Two Abodes: Refutation of the Two Sects, Wahhabis and Zahiri Followers"].

Al-Saqqaf al-Shafi`i, Hasan ibn `Ali, Islamic Research Intitute, Amman, Jordan: *al-Ighatha bi adillat al-istighatha wa al-radd al-mubin `ala munkiri al-tawassul* ["The Mercy of God in the Proofs of Seeking Intercession and the Clear Answer to Those who Reject it"]; *Ilqam al hajar li al-mutatawil `ala al-Asha`ira min al-Bashar* ["The Stoning of All Those Who Attack Ash'aris"]; *Qamus shata'im al-Albani wa al-alfaz al-munkara al-lati yatluquha fi haqq ulama al-ummah wa fudalai'ha wa ghayrihim...* ["Encyclopedia of al-Albani's Abhorrent Expressions Which He Uses Against the Scholars of the Community, its Eminent Men, and Others..."] Amman : Dar al-Imam al-Nawawi, 1993.

Al-Sawi al-Misri: *Hashiyat `ala al-jalalayn* ["Commentary on the Tafsir of the Two Jalal al-Din"].

Sayf al-Din Ahmed ibn Muhammad: *Al-Albani Unveiled: An Exposition of His Errors and Other Important Issues*, 2nd ed. (London: s.n., 1994).

Al-Shatti al-Athari al-Hanbali, al-Sayyid Mustafa ibn Ahmad ibn Hasan, Mufti of Syria: *al-Nuqul al-shar'iyyah fi al-radd 'ala al-Wahhabiyya* ["The Legal Proofs in Answering the Wahhabis"].

Al-Subki, al-hafiz Taqi al-Din (d. 756/1355): *Al-durra al-mudiyya fi al-radd `ala Ibn Taymiyya*, ed. Muhammad Zahid al-Kawthari ["The Luminous Pearl: A Refutation of Ibn Taymiyya"]; *Al-rasa'il al-subkiyya fi al-radd `ala Ibn Taymiyya wa tilmidhihi Ibn Qayyim al-Jawziyya*, ed. Kamal al-Hut ["Subki's treatises in Answer to Ibn Taymiyya and his pupil Ibn Qayyim al-Jawziyya"] (Beirut: `Alam al-Kutub, 1983); *Al-sayf al-saqil fi al-radd `ala Ibn Zafil* ["The Burnished Sword in Refuting Ibn Zafil (Ibn Qayyim al-Jawziyya)" Cairo: Matba`at al-Sa`ada, 1937; *Shifa' al-siqam fi ziyarat khayr al-anam* ["The healing of the sick in visiting the Best of Creation"].

Sunbul al-Hanafi al-Ta'ifi, Allama Tahir: *Sima al-Intisar lil awliya' al-abrar* ["The Mark of Victory Belongs to Allah's Pure Friends"].

Al-Tabataba'i al-Basri, al-Sayyid: also wrote a reply to San`a'i's poem which was excerpted in Samnudi's *Sa`adat al-Darayn*. After reading it, San`a'i reversed his position and said: "I have repented from what I said concerning the Najdi."

Al-Tamimi al-Maliki, `Allama Isma`il (d. 1248), Shaykh al-Islam in Tunis: wrote a refutation of a treatise of Ibn `Abd al-Wahhab.

Al-Wazzani, al-Shaykh al-Mahdi, Mufti of Fes, Morocco: Wrote a refutation of Muhammad `Abduh's prohibition of tawassul.

al-Zahawi al-Baghdadi, Jamil Effendi Sidqi (d. 1355/1936): *al-Fajr al-Sadiq fi al-radd 'ala munkiri al-tawassul wa al-khawariq* ["The True Dawn in Refuting Those Who Deny the Seeking of Intercession and the Miracles of Saints"] Pub. 1323/1905 in Egypt.

Al-Zamzami al-Shafi`i, Muhammad Salih, Imam of the Maqam Ibrahim in Mecca, wrote a book in 20 chapters against them according to al-Sayyid al-Haddad.

See also:
Ahmad, Qeyamuddin. *The Wahhabi movement in India.* 2nd rev. ed. New Delhi : Manohar, 1994.

AHADITH ON THE KHAWARIJ WHICH THE SCHOLARS CONSIDER TO APPLY TO THE WAHHABIS

These ahadith are cited in the Six Books of authentic traditions for the most part. They have been collated for the most part from the following two books written in refutation of the Wahhabi heresy:

a) al-Sayyid al-`Alawi ibn Ahmad ibn Hasan ibn `Abd Allah ibn `Alawi al-Haddad: *Misbah al-anam wa jala' al-zalam fi radd shubah al-bid`i al-Najdi al-lati adalla biha al- `awamm* ["The Lamp of Creatures and the Illumination of Darkness Concerning the Refutation of the Errors of the Innovator From Najd by Which He Had Misled the Common People"] published 1325H.

b) al-Sayyid Ahmad ibn Zayni al-Dahlan (d. 1304/1886). Mufti of Mecca and Shaykh al-Islam in the Hijaz region of the Ottoman state: *Khulasat al-kalam fi bayan umara' al-balad al-haram* ["The Summation Concerning the Leaders of the Holy Sanctuary"] (A History of the Wahhabi Fitna in Najd and the Hijaz) p. 234-236.

The Prophet said, Peace be upon him:

1. "They [Khawarij = those outside] transferred the Qur'anic verses meant to refer to unbelievers and made them refer to believers."

2. "What I most fear in my community is a man who interprets verses of the Qur'an out of context."

3. "The confusion [fitna] comes from there (and he pointed to the East = Najd in present-day Eastern Saudi Arabia)."

4. "A people that recite Qur'an will come out of the East, but it will not go past their throats. They will pass through the religion (of Islam) like the arrow passes through its quarry. They will no more come back to the religion than the arrow will come back to its course. Their sign is that they shave (their heads)."

5. "There will be in my Community a dissent and a faction, a people with excellent words and vile deeds. They will read Qur'an, but their faith does not go past their throats. They will pass through religion the way an arrow passes through its quarry. They will no more come back to the religion than the arrow will come back to its original course. They are the worst of human beings and the worst of all creation. The one who kills them or is killed by them is blessed. They summon to the book of Allah but they have nothing to do with it. Whoever kills them is closer to Allah than they. Their sign is that they shave (their heads)."

6. "A people will come out at the end of times, immature, foolish and corrupt. They will hold the discourse of the best of creation and recite Qur'an, but it will not go past their throats. They will passes through religion the way an arrow passes through its quarry. If you find them, kill them, for verily whoever kills them will have his reward from Allah the Day of Judgment."

7. "There will be people in my Community whose mark is that they shave (their heads). They will recite Qur'an, but it will not go past their throats. They will pass through religion the way an arrow passes through its target. They are the worst of human beings and the worst of all creation."

8. "The apex of disbelief is towards the East [Najd]. Pride and arrogance is found among the people of the horse and the camel [Bedouin Arabs]."

9. "Harshness and dryness of heart are in the East [Najd], and true belief is among the people of Hijaz."

10. "O Allah, bless us in our Syria and in our Yemen!" They said: "Ya Rasulallah, and in our Najd!" He didn't reply. He blessed Syria and Yemen twice more. They asked him to bless Najd twice more but he didn't reply. The third time he said: "There [in Najd] are the earthquakes and the dissensions, and through it will dawn the epoch [or horn] of shaytan."

11. A version has, "The two epochs [or horns] of shaytan." Some scholars have said that the dual referred to Musaylima the Arch-liar and to Muhammad ibn `Abd al-Wahhab.

12. Some versions continue with the words: "And in it [Najd] is the consuming disease," i.e. death.

13. Some books of history mention the following version in the chapters devoted to the battles against the Banu Hanifa:
"At the end of times a man will come out of Musaylima's country and he will change the religion of Islam." Note: Most of the Khawarij were from the Najd area, from the tribes of Banu Hanifa, Banu Tamim, and Wa'il. Musaylima was from the Banu Hanifa, and Ibn `Abd al-Wahhab is from Tamim.

13a. Abu Bakr said concerning the Banu Hanifa (the tribe of Musaylima the Liar): "Their valley [Najd] will not cease to be a valley of dissensions until the end of time, and the religion will never recover from their liars until Judgment Day," and in another version: "Woe to al-Yamama without end."

13b. When `Ali killed the Khawarij, someone said: "Praise be to Allah Who has brought them down and relieved us from them." Ali replied: "Verily, by the One in Whose hand is my soul, some of them are still in the loins of men and they have not been born yet, and the last of them will fight on the side of the Antichrist."

14. "A people that recite the Qur'an will come out of the East, but it will not go past their throats. Every time a generation of them is cut down another one will come until the last one finds itself on the side of the Antichrist."

15. "There will be a huge confusion within my Community. There will not remain one house of the Arabs except that confusion will enter it. Those who die because of it are in the fire. The harm of the tongue in it will be greater than that of the sword."

16. "There will be a dissension (in which people will be) deaf, dumb and blind (this means they will be blind and not see the true issue nor listen to the voice of truth): whoever tries to control it, the dissension will control him."

17. "A shaytan will appear in Najd by whose dissension the Arabian island will quake."

18. On the authority of al-`Abbas: "A man will come out in the twelfth century in the Wadi Abu Hanifah [in Najd] (whose appearance is) like a bull that lunges against its yoke. There will be much slaughter and killing in his time. They will make the possessions of Muslims lawful for themselves and for trade among themselves. They will make the lives of Muslims lawful for themselves and for boasting among themselves. In that confusion the despised and the lowly will attain positions of power. Their idle desires will keep company with them the way a dog keeps company with its master."

19. On the authority of Abu Sa`id al-Khudri: "Verily in the wake of this time of mine comes a people who will recite Qur'an but it will not go past their throats. They will pass through religion the way an arrow passes through its quarry. They will kill the Muslims and leave the idolaters alone. If I saw them, verily I would kill them the way the tribe of `Aad was killed [i.e. all of them]."

20. "There will be towards the end of time a people who will say to you what neither you nor your forebears ever heard before. Beware of them lest they misguide you and bring you confusion."

21. "They will pass through Islam like an arrow passes through its quarry. Wherever you meet them, kill them!"

22. "They are the dogs of the people of Hell."

23. "They recite Qur'an and consider it in their favor but it is against them."

24. "There will be thirty dajjals (antichrists) after me, all claiming prophethood."

25. "Some people will be standing and calling at the gates of hell; whoever responds to their call, their will throw him into the Fire. They will be from our own people [i.e. Arabs] and will speak our language [Arabic]. Should you live to see them, stick to the main body *(jama`a)* of the Muslims and their leader. (If there is no main body and no leader,) isolate yourself from all these sects, even if you have to eat from the roots of trees until death overcomes you while you are in that state."

26. "Just before the Hour there will be many liars." Jabir ibn Samurah said: "Be on your guard against them."

27. "The Hour will not come until thirty dajjals appear, all of them lying about Allah and His Messenger."

28. "There will be Dajjals and liars among my Community. They will tell you something new, which neither you nor your forefathers have heard. Be on your guard against them and do not let them lead you astray."

29. "The time of the Dajjal will be years of confusion. People will believe a liar, and disbelieve one who tells the truth. People will distrust one who is trustworthy, and trust one who is treacherous; and the *ruwaybidha* will have a say." Someone asked: "Who are they?" He said: "Those who rebel against Allah and will have a say in general affairs."

30. "If the leadership is entrusted to those unfit for it, expect the Hour."

31. "You will see the barefoot ones, the naked, the destitute, the shepherds and camelherds take pride in building tall structures in abundance."

32. "One of the signs of the change of religion is the affectation of eloquence by the rabble and their betaking to palaces in big cities."

Jamil Effendi al-Zahawi's

al-Fajr al-sadiq fi al-radd `ala munkiri al-tawassul wa al-khawariq

"The True Dawn: A Refutation of Those Who Deny The Validity of Using Means to God and the Miracles of Saints"

1: The Origin of the Wahhabi Sect The Wahhabiyya is a sect whose origin can be traced back to Muhammad Ibn `Abd al-Wahhab. Although he first came on the scene in 1143 (1730 CE), the subversive current his false doctrine initiated took some fifty years to spread. It first showed up in Najd. This is the same district that produced the false prophet, Musaylima in the early days of Islam. Muhammad Ibn Sa`ud, governor of this district, aided Ibn `Abd al-Wahhab's effort, forcing people to follow him. One Arab tribe after another allowed itself to be deceived until sedition became commonplace in the region, his notoriety grew and his power soon passed beyond anyone's control. The nomadic Arabs of the surrounding desert feared him. He used to say to the people: "I call upon you but to confess *tawhid* (monotheism) and to avoid *shirk* (associating partners with God in worship)." The people of the countryside followed him and where he walked, they walked until his dominance increased.

Muhammad Ibn `Abd al-Wahhab was born in 1111 and died in 1207 (1699-1792 CE). At the outset of his career, he used to go back and forth to Mecca and Madina in quest of knowledge. In Madina, he studied with Shaykh Muhammad Ibn Sulayman al-Kurdi and Shaykh Muhammad Hayat al-Sindi (d. 1750). These two shaykhs as well as others with whom he studied early on detected the heresy of Ibn `Abd al-Wahhab's creed. They used to say: "God will allow him be led astray; but even unhappier will be the lot of those misled by him." Circumstances had reached this state when his father `Abd al-Wahhab, a pious scholars of the religion, detected heresy in his belief and began to warn others about his son. His own brother Sulayman soon followed suit, going so far as to write a book entitled *al-Sawa`iq* (the thunderbolts)[3] to refute the innovative and subversive creed manufactured by Ibn `Abd al-Wahhab.

Famous writers of the day made a point of noting the similarity between Ibn `Abd al-Wahhab's beginnings and those of the false prophets prominent in Islam's initial epoch like Musaylima the Prevaricator, Sajah al-Aswad al-Anasi, Tulaiha al-Asadi and others of their kind.[4] What was different in `Abd al-Wahhab's case was his concealment in himself of any outright claim to prophecy. Undoubtedly, he was unable to gain support enough to openly proclaim it. Nevertheless, he would call those who came from abroad to join his movement *Muhajirun* and those who came from his own region *Ansar* in patent imitation of those who took flight from Mecca with the Prophet Muhammad in contrast to the inhabitants of Madina at the start of Islam. Ibn `Abd al-Wahhab habitually ordered anyone who had already made the obligatory Pilgrimage (Hajj) to Mecca prior joining him to remake it since God had not accepted it the first time they performed because they had done so as unbelievers. He was also given to telling people wishing to enter his religion: "You must bear witness against yourself that you were a disbeliever and you must bear witness against your parents that they were disbelievers and died as such."

---

[3]Sulayman ibn `abd al-Wahhab al-Najdi, *al-Sawa'iq al-Ilahiyya fi al-radd 'ala al-Wahhabiyya* ["Divine Lightnings in Refuting the Wahhabis"], ed. Ibrahim Muhammad al-Batawi (Cairo: dar al-insan, 1987). Offset reprint by Waqf Ikhlas, Istanbul: Hakikat Kitabevi, 1994.

[4]These were self-declared prophets in the time of the Prophet and directly after.

His practice was to declare a group of famous scholars of the past unbelievers. If a potential recruit to his movement agreed and testified to the truth of that declaration, he was accepted; if not, an order was given and he was summarily put to death. Ibn `Abd al-Wahhab made no secret of his view that the Muslim community had existed for the last six hundred years in a state of unbelief *(kufr)* and he said the same of whoever did not follow him. Even if a person was the most pious and God-fearing of Muslims, he would denounce them as idolaters *(mushrikun)*, thus making the shedding of their blood and confiscation of their wealth licit *(halal)*.

On the other hand, he affirmed the faith of anyone who followed him even though they be persons of most notoriously corrupt and profligate styles of life. He played always on a single theme: the dignity to which God had entitled him. This directly corresponded to the decreased reverence he claimed was due the Prophet whose status as Messenger he frequently depreciated using language fit to describe an errand boy rather than a divinely commissioned apostle of faith. He would say such things as "I looked up the account of Hudaybiyya and found it to contain this or that lie." He was in the habit of using contemptuous speech of this kind to the point that one follower felt free to say in his actual presence: "This stick in my hand is better than Muhammad because it benefits me by enabling me to walk. But Muhammad is dead and benefits me not at all". This, of course, expresses nothing less than disbelief and counts legally as such in the fours schools of Islamic law.[5]

Returning always to the same theme, Ibn `Abd al-Wahhab used to say that prayer for the Prophet was reprehensible and disliked *(makruh)* in the Shari`a. He would prohibit blessings on the Prophet from being recited on the eve of Friday prayer and their public utterance from the minbar, and punish harshly anyone who

---

[5]It is an offense passible of death to disparage the Prophet in all Four Schools according to the ijma`. See the chapters on disparaging the Prophet in Qadi `Iyad's *Shifa'*, Ibn Taymiyya's *Al-sarim al-maslul*, Ibn Qunfudh's *Wasilat al-islam bi al-nabi*, etc.

pronounced such blessings. He even went so far as to kill a blind *mu'adhdhin* (caller to prayer) who did not cease and desist when he commanded him to abandon praying for the Prophet in the conclusion to his call to prayer. He deceived his followers by saying that all that was done to keep monotheism pure.

At the same time, he burned many books containing prayers for the Prophet, among them Dala'il al-Khayrat and others, similar in content and theme. In this fashion, he destroyed countless books on Islamic law, commentary on the Qur'an, and the science of hadith whose common fault lay in their contradiction of his own vacuous creed. While doing this, however, he never ceased encouraging any follower to interpret Qur'an and hadith for himself and to execute this informed only by the light of his own understanding, darkened though it be through errant belief and heretical indoctrination.

Ibn `Abd al-Wahhab clung fiercely to denouncing people as unbelievers. To do this he used Qur'anic verses originally revealed about idolaters and extended their application to monotheists. It has been narrated by `Abd Allah Ibn `Umar and recorded by Imam Bukhari in his book of sound hadiths that the Khawarij transferred the Qur'anic verses meant to refer to unbelievers and made them refer to believers.[6] He also relates another narration transmitted on the authority of Ibn `Umar whereby the Prophet, on him be peace, said: "What I most fear in my community is a man who interprets verses of the Qur'an out of context." The latter hadith and the one preceding it apply to the case of Ibn `Abd al-Wahhab and his followers.

It is obvious the intention to found a new religion lay behind his statements and actions. In consequence, the only thing he accepted from the religion of our Prophet, on him be peace was the Qur'an. Yet even this was a matter of surface show. It allowed people to be ignorant of what his aims really were. Indicating this is the way he and his followers used to interpret the Qur'an according

---

[6]Bukhari, English ed. 9:50.

to their own whim and ignore the commentary provided by the Prophet, on him be peace, his Companions, the pious predecessors of our Faith *(al-salaf al-salihun)*, and the Imams of Qur'anic commentary. He did not argue on the strength of the narrations of the Prophet and sayings of the Companions, the Successors to the Companions and the Imams among those who derived rulings in the Shari`a by means of ijtihad nor did he adjudicate legal cases on the basis of the principle sources *(usul)* of the Shari`a; that is, he did not adhere to Consensus *(ijma`)* nor to sound analogy *(qiyas)*. Although he claimed to belong to the legal school *(madhhab)* of Imam Ahmad Ibn Hanbal, this pretense was motivated by falsehood and dissimulation. The scholars and jurists of the Hanbali school rejected his multifarious errors. They wrote numerous articles refuting him including his brother whose book touching on Ibn `Abd al-Wahhab's errors was mentioned earlier.

The learned Sayyid al-Haddad al-Alawi[7] said: "In our opinion, the one element in the statements and actions of Ibn `Abd al-Wahhab that makes his departure from the foundations of Islam unquestionable is the fact that he, without support of any generally accepted interpretation of Qur'an or Sunna *(bi la ta'wil)*, takes matters in our religion necessarily well-known to be objects of prohibition *(haram)* agreed upon by consensus *(ijma`)* and makes them permissible *(halal)*.[8] Furthermore, along with that he disparages the prophets, the messengers, saints and the pious. Willful disparagement of anyone failing under these categories of person is unbelief *(kufr)* according to the consensus reached by the four Imams of the schools of Islamic law.

Then he wrote an essay called "The Clarification of Unclarity Concerning the Creator of Heaven and Earth" *(kashf al-shubuhat `an khaliq al-ardi wa al-samawat)*[9] for Ibn Sa`ud. In this

---

[7]This is the father of al-Habib Ahmad Mashhur al-Haddad who died in Mecca in 1995 -- may God have mercy on both of them.

[8]E.g. asking Muslims to repeat their shahada, or killing them.

[9]Edited by `Abd Allah ibn `Abd al-Rahman Al Bassam, 1st ed. (Cairo: Dar ihya al-kutub al-`arabiyah, 1377 [1957 or 1958]).

work he declared that all present-day Muslims are disbelievers and have been so for the last six hundred years. He applied the verses in the Qur'an, meant to refer to disbelievers among the tribe of the Quraysh to most God-fearing and pious individuals of the Muslim community. Ibn Sa`ud naturally took this work as a pretext and device for extending his political sovereignty by subjecting the Arabs to his dominance. Ibn `Abd al-Wahhab began to call people to his religion and instilled in their hearts the idea that every one under the sun was an idolater. What's more, anyone who slew an idolater, when he died, would go immediately to paradise.

As a consequence, Ibn Sa`ud carried out whatever Ibn `Abd al-Wahhab ordered. If he commanded him to kill someone and seize his property, he hastened to do just that. Indeed, Ibn `Abd al-Wahhab sat among his folk like a prophet in the midst of his community. His people did not forsake one jot or little of what he told them to do and acted only as he commanded, magnifying him to the highest degree and honoring him in every conceivable way. The clans and tribes of the Arabs continued to magnify him in this manner until, by that means, the dominion of Ibn Sa`ud increased far and wide as well as that of his sons after him.

The Sharif of Mecca, Ghalib, waged war against Ibn Sa`ud for fifteen years until he grew too old and weak to fight. No one remained if his supporters except they joined the side of his foe. It was then that Ibn Sa`ud entered Mecca in a negotiated peace settlement in the year 1220 (1805 CE). There he abided for some seven years until the Sublime Porte (i.e. the Ottoman government) raised a military force addressing command to its minister, the honorable Muhammad `Ali Pasha, ruler of Egypt. His intrepid army advanced against Ibn Sa`ud and cleared the land of him and his followers. Then, he summoned his son Ibrahim Pasha who arrived in the district in the year 1233 (1818 CE). He finished off what remained of them.

Among the hideous abominations of Ibn `Abd al-Wahhab was his prohibiting people from visiting the tomb of the Prophet, on him be God's blessing and peace. After his prohibition, a group went out from Ahsa to visit the Prophet. When they returned, they passed by Ibn `Abd al-Wahhab in the district and he commanded that their beards be shaved and they be saddled on their mounts backwards to return in this fashion to Ahsa. The Prophet, on him be peace, related information about those Khawarij preserved in numerous hadiths. Indeed, these sayings constitute one of the signs of his prophethood; for they convey knowledge of the unseen. Among them are his statements in Bukhari and Muslim: "Discord there; discord there!" pointing to the East; and "A people will come out of the East who will read Qur'an with it not getting past their throats. They will pass through the religion like an arrow when it passes clean through the flesh of its quarry and comes back pristine and prepared to be shot once again from the bow. They will bear a sign in the shaving of their heads." Another narration of the hadith adds: "They are calamity for the whole of God's creation; Blessed is he who kills them" or "Slay them! For though they appeal to God's Book, they have no share therein." He said: O God! bless us in our Syria and bless us in our Yemen!" They said: O Messenger of God! And in our Najd? but he replied: In Najd will occur earthquakes and discords; in it will dawn the epoch [or horn] of Shaytan." Again he said: "A people will come out of the East, reading the Qur'an and yet it will not get past their throats. Whenever one generation is cut off, another arises until the last dawns with the coming of Antichrist. They will bear a sign in the shaving of their heads."

Now the Prophet's words explicitly specify in text his reference to those people coming out of the East, following Ibn `Abd al-Wahhab in the innovations he made in Islam. For they were in the habit of ordering those who followed them to shave their heads and once they began to follow them, they did not abandon this practice. In none of the sects of the past prior to that of Ibn `Abd al-Wahhab did the likes of this practice occur.[10] He even

---

[10]The mufti of Zabid (Yemen) al-Sayyid Abd al-Rahman al-Ahdal said: "It is enough testimony against Muhammad ibn Abd al-Wahhab that the Prophet (s) said: "Their mark is that they shave," for this was never done by any of the sects of innovators before him."

ordered the women who followed him to shave their heads. Once he ordered a woman who entered his new religion to shave her head. She replied: " If you ordered men to shave off their beards, then it would be permissible for you to order a woman to shave her head. But the hair on a woman's head has the same sacred status as a man's beard." Ibn `Abd al-Wahhab was unable to answer her.

Found among the narrations transmitted from the Prophet, on him be peace, is his statement: "At the end of time, a man will rise up in the same region from which once rose Musaylima. He would change the religion of Islam." Another saying has it: "From Najd a Shaytan will appear on the scene causing the Arab peninsula to erupt in earthquake from discord and strife."

One of the abominations of Ibn `Abd al-Wahhab was his burning of books containing works of Islamic science and his slaughter of the scholars of our faith and people both of the top classes and common people. He made the shedding of their blood and confiscation of their property and wealth licit well as digging up graves of awliya (saints). In Ahsa, for example, he ordered that some of the graves of awliya be used by people to relieve the wants of nature. He forbade people to read Imam Jazuli's *Dala'il al-Khayrat*, to perform supererogatory acts of devotion, to utter the names of God in His remembrance, to read the mawlid celebrating the Prophet's birth, or to evoke blessings and prayers on the Prophet from the Minaret after the call to prayer. What's more, he killed whoever dared to do any of those things. He forbade any kind of act of worship after the canonical prayers. He would publicly declare a Muslim a disbeliever for requesting a prophet,

---

Related by al- Sayyid Ahmad Dahlan in his book *Khulasat al-kalam fi bayan umara' al-balad al-haram* p. 235.

When Ibn `Abd al-Wahhab had a group of Muslims killed because they did not shave their heads as he required his followers to do, al-Mun`ami wrote a lampoon whose first verse is:

Afi halqi al-ra'si bis sakakina wal haddi
hadithun sahihun bil asanida `an jaddi

[Is there, concerning shaving the head at swordpoint,
an authentic hadith related from my ancestor the Prophet?]

angel or individual of saintly life to join his or her prayers to that person's own prayer expressing some intention whose fulfillment might be asked of God as, for example, when one supplicates the Creator for the sake of Muhammad, on him be peace, to accomplish such-and-such a need. He also said anyone who addressed a person as lord or master *(sayyid)* was a disbeliever.

Undoubtedly, one of the worst abominations perpetrated by the Wahhabis under the leadership of Ibn `Abd al-Wahhab was the massacre of the people of Ta'if. upon entering that town. They killed everyone in sight, slaughtering both child and adult, the ruler and the ruled, the lowly and well-born. They began with a suckling child nursing at his mother's breast and moved on to a group studying Qur'an, slaying them, down to the last man. And when they wiped out the people they found in the houses, they went out into the streets, the shops and the mosques, killing whoever happened to be there. They killed even men bowed in prayer until they had annihilated every Muslim who dwelt in Ta'if and only a remnant, some twenty or more, remained.

These were holed up in Beit al-Fitni with ammunition, inaccessible to their approach. There was another group at Beit al-Far to the number of two-hundred and seventy who fought them that day, then the second and third until the Wahhabis sent them a guarantee of clemency; only they tendered this proposal as a trick. For when they entered, they seized their weapons and slew them to a man. Others, they also brought out with a guarantee of clemency and a pact to the valley of Waj where they abandoned them in the cold and snow, barefoot, naked exposed in shame with their women, accustomed to the privacy afforded them by common decency and religious morality. They, then, plundered their possessions: wealth of any kind, household furnishings and cash.

They cast books into the streets alleys and byways to be blown to and fro by the wind among which could be found copies of the Qur'an, volumes of Bukhari, Muslim, other canonical collections of hadith and books of fiqh, all mounting to the thousands. These books remained there for several days, trampled upon by the Wahhabis. What's more, no one among them made the slightest attempt to remove even one page of Qur'an from under foot to preserve it from the ignominy of this display of disrespect. Then, they raised the houses and made what was once a town a barren waste land. That was in the year 1217 (1802 CE).

2: The Wahhabis and their Recent Rebellion (1905)

The leader of the Wahhabis at the time of the present account is `Abd al-Rahman Ibn Faysal, one of the sons of Muhammad Ibn Sa`ud, the Rebel who turned his face in disobedience to the greater Islamic Caliphate in the year 1205 (1790 CE). The incidents he occasioned with the Sharif of Mecca, Ghalib continued up to 1220 (1805 CE). Then, when the Sharif's power to do battle with him waned, the Sublime Porte raised a military force against him, charging its minister the late Muhammad `Ali Pasha, ruler of Egypt, and his son, the late Ibrahim Pasha, with its command as we pointed out in the preceding chapter just as books of history have written it down.

Now this `Abd al-Rahman was for almost thirty years governor of Riyadh. Then, Muhammad Ibn al-Rashid, took over Najd as its governor and Ibn Sa`ud fled to the remote areas by the sea coast. He ultimately ended up in Kuwait where he remained in humiliating poverty. Nor did anyone feel sorry for him until the Sublime Porte looked on him with favor and afforded him a remittance. Thereupon, he began to live a more comfortable life, though in a state of exile, due to the largesse of the Ottoman government.

When Muhammad Ibn al Rashid died, May God have mercy on his soul, his nephew came to power, `Abd al-Aziz Ibn Mut'ab Ibn al-Rashid, who is governor of Najd at the time of writing this. It fell out that an incident took place between the `Abd al-Aziz just mentioned and the Shaykh of Kuwait, Mubarak Ibn Sabah. Behind it was Mubarak Ibn Sabah's murder of his brother, Muhammad Ibn Sabah who was, at that time, *locum tenens* or temporary substitute of the Sublime Porte in Kuwait. The same individual also murdered his other brother and robbed his children of an immense inheritance. The latter heirs, thereupon, fled the fratricide's further pursuit. Faced with this state affairs, the uncle of the murdered children, Yusuf Ibn Ibrahim, took refuge with `Abd al-Aziz Ibn al-Rashid, the Governor of Najd, taking sides in his presence against his own brother Mubarak Ibn Sabah, the aforementioned fratricide, in an attempt get back the wealth the latter had robbed from his nephews.

Negotiations of reconciliation broke down to the point that each of the two parties in the dispute fitted out an army, one against the other. The two armies clashed at a place called Tarafiya. Mubarak Ibn Sabah suffered defeat and some four thousands fighters from his army were killed, although he escaped unharmed. He fled back to Kuwait vanquished and humiliated. However, no time elapsed before Ibn Sabah sought foreign protection and rebelled again. The foreigners supplied both money and arms. Then, the power of `Abd al-Rahman ibn Faysal ibn Sa`ud began to wax strong against the Governor of Najd, al-Rashid. It chanced that the latter was at that moment preoccupied by military expeditions in the remote districts of Riyadh.

Mubarak Ibn Sabah seized his opportunity. Helped by foreigners with money and weapons, he fitted out an army and placed it under the command of that `Abd al-Rahman mentioned earlier. Ibn Sabah dispatched him to Riyadh to capture it, occupy it by force, fortify its barriers and entrench himself within. When the news of what had happened reached the governor, Ibn al-Rashid, he returned and encircled it for a time with the intent of taking it back. His encampment around Riyadh lasted for a year. Then, something occurred in one of remote areas of the district that distracted him from the encirclement and he abandoned it. This afforded Ibn Sa`ud an opportunity as well, for he came out with his army outfitted with foreign aid and seized `Unayza, Burayda, and the remainder of the regions of Qusaym.

The Sublime Porte witnessed the hostile action of `Abd al-Rahman, his rebellion and insolence against its friend the faithful

Governor of Najd, Ibn al-Rashid, as well as his defection to the foreigner, it dispatched a squadron from its intrepid armies as a support for the Governor of Najd, Ibn al-Rashid to cut off the rear end of those renegades and crush their hostile activities. Ibn al-Rashid snuffed out the sparks of sedition. The Ottoman forces clashed with the rebels, the party of Ibn Sa`ud near the town of Bahkrama in the region of Qusaym. A fierce battle between the two forces ensued, issuing finally in the defeat of the rebellious party, the forces of Ibn Sa`ud. The victorious army took possession of eleven standards of their defeated foe. Ibn al-Rashid and his soldiers were extolled for their role in crushing the enemy in this battle and their bravery; the memory of it will last forever. This praise has an undeniable base in fact, word and deed. [At the time of writing this,] the vanquished are presently enclosed and surrounded with the intrepid forces of Ibrahim Pasha looking on and encompassing them round about, praised for their exemplary manner of containing the enemy and curbing his defiance.

3: The Wahhabi Creed

When Ibn `Abd al-Wahhab saw that the inhabitants of the rural regions of Najd were different from the urbane world of its cities, he would extol the simplicity and innocence of human beings as they are found in the primordial state of the Arabs. Ignorance, then, gained the upper hand among the city-dwellers so that sciences of an intellectual character lost status in their eyes. Besides, there was no longer an appetite in their hearts for things sound and wholesome, once he had sewn in their hearts the seeds of corruption and vice. For it was to vice and corruption that his own soul had become attuned since time immemorial nourished by his grab at political leadership masked under the name of religion. After all, he believed -- May God revile him -- that prophethood was only a matter of political leadership which the cleverest people attain when circumstances help them in the form of an ignorant and uninformed crowd.

Moreover, since God the Exalted had shut tight the door of prophecy after the Seal of the Prophets, our master Muhammad, on him be God's blessing and peace, there was no way to realize the goal of his desires except to claim that he was a renewer of the faith *(mujaddid)* and an independent thinker in the formulation of legal rulings *(mujtahid)*. Such an attitude -- or rather the worst and most profound state of moral misguidance and religious disbelief -- brought him to the point of declaring every group of Muslims disbelievers and idolaters. For he set out to apply the verses of Qur'an specifically revealed to single out the idolaters of the Arabs to generally include all Muslims who visit the grave of their Prophet, and seek his intercession with their Lord.

In doing this, he cast aside what ran counter to his own invalid claims and the vain desires commanding his ego to work mischief regarding the explicit statements of the Master of all messengers and Imams, the mujtahids of our religion (that is, who have the capacity to exercise independent reasoning in the process of legal discovery). Hence, when he saw a consensus of legal opinion in matters of faith which clashed with his own unwarranted innovations, he rejected it as a matter of principle, asserting: "I do not entertain any opinion of people coming after the Qur'an which contains all that pertains to Islam, the fresh and the dry (cf. 6: 59)." Thus, he failed to heed what the Qur'an itself declared, when it says: "He who follows the path of those other than the Muslims" (4:115) inasmuch as he accepted from Qur'an only what it reveals concerning the idolaters of the Arabs. These verses he interpreted in his own obscure fashion, having the gall to stand before God and facilitate the accomplishment of his own personal political ambitions by means of an unwarranted and unjustified exegesis of His holy text. His method here mostly consisted in applying these verses concerning the idolaters to Muslims and on this basis declaring that they had been disbeliever for the last six hundred years, that one may shed their blood with impunity and confiscate their property and reduce their land, the Abode of Peace, *(Dar al-Islam)* to a field of war against disbelief *(Dar al-Harb)*.

Yet the Prophet, on him be God's blessings and peace, from what we see in the two canonical collections of sound hadith, Bukhari and Muslim, declared in the narration where the angel

Jibril assumes human form to question him about the creed of Islam: "Islam is to testify that there is no god but God and Muhammad is the Messenger of God." Again, in the narration of `Umar he says: "Islam is built upon five articles of faith (the first being): "Testimony that there is no god but God, Muhammad is His servant and Messenger." Then, there is his declaration to the delegation of `Abd al-Qays also cited in Bukhari and Muslim: "I am commanding you to believe in God alone. Do you know what belief in God alone is? It is to testify: "There is no god but God and Muhammad is the Messenger of God."" Also cited is his exhortation: "I have been ordered to fight people until they say: "There is no god but God and that Muhammad is the Messenger of God." Finally, the Prophet says: "It is sufficient that folk say: "There is no god but God."

However, Ibn `Abd al-Wahhab and his followers go counter to all these statements of the Prophet, on him be peace. They make a disbeliever the one who says: "There is no god but God and Muhammad is the Messenger of God" because that person is not like them in respect to their claim that the one who testifies in the aforementioned fashion and yet asks God for something for the sake of a prophet or evokes the name of someone absent or dead or makes a vow to that person it is as if his belief diverges from his testimony. His only aim here is to market goods unsaleable where sound hadiths and correct exegeses of the Qur'an are exchanged. We will explain -- God willing -- the groundlessness of this claim and show its spuriousness to the reader.

It is amazing how Ibn `Abd al-Wahhab misrepresents use of the prophet's name in petitions to God or tawassul under the pretense of monotheism *(tawhid)* and divine transcendence *(tanzih)* claiming that use of a prophet's name in this manner constitutes association of a partner with God; yet at the same time there is his outright assertion to the effect that God's mounting His throne is like sitting on it and his affirmation that God has a hand, face and possesses spatial dimension! He says it is possible to point to Him in the sky and claims that He literally descends to the lower heavens so that he gives a body to God who is too exalted in the height of

His sublimity beyond what obscurantists proclaim. What happens to Divine transcendence after making God a body so that the lowliest of inanimate creatures share properties in common with their Creator? To what is He, the Exalted, transcendent when He is characterized in so deprecating a fashion and His divinity couched in terms so redolent of ridicule and contempt?

One of Ibn `Abd al-Wahhab's more enormous stupidities is this: When he sees reason going against his claims, he casts aside all modesty and suspends reason giving it no role in his judgment. He endeavors thereby to make people like dumb beasts when it comes to matters of faith. He prohibits reason to enter into religious affairs despite the fact that there is no contradiction between reason and faith. On the contrary, whenever human minds reach their full measure of completeness and perfection, religion's merits and prerogatives with regard to reason become totally manifest. Is there in this age, an age of the mind's progress, anything more abominable than denying reason its proper scope, especially when the cardinal pivot of religion and the capacity to perform its duties is based on the ability to reason? For the obligation to carry out the duties of Islam falls away when mental capacity is absent. God has addressed his servants in many places in the Qur'an: "O you who possess understanding" (cf. 65:10) alerting them to the fact that knowledge of the realities of religion is only a function of those possessed of minds.

Now the time has come for me to give a summation of the vain and empty prattle of the renegade Wahhabi sect which it aspires to issue as a doctrine. Next, I shall discuss it in terms of the research that has been brought in its rebuttal and refute its argument. Their invalid creed consists of a number of articles:

(1) Affirming the face, hand, and spatial direction of the Creator and making Him a body that descends and ascends;
(2) Making principles derived from narration *(naql)* prior to those derived from reason *(`aql)*;
(3) Denial and rejection of consensus as a principle *(asl)* of Shari`a legislation;

(4) Similar denial and rejection of analogy *(qiyas)*;
(5) Not permitting copying and emulating the judgments of the Imams who have in Islam the status of those capable of exercising independent reasoning in matters of Shari`a;
(6) Declaring Muslims who contradict them disbelievers;
(7) Prohibition of using the name of the Messenger in petitions to God or the name of someone else among the friends of God and the pious;
(8) Making the visiting of the tombs of prophets and of pious people illicit;
(9) Declaring a Muslim a disbeliever who makes a vow to someone other than God or sacrifices at the grave or final resting place of awliya or the pious.

4: Their Making God Into A Body *(Tajsim)*

Although the Wahhabis declare any Muslim a disbeliever who visits the Prophet's grave and asks God for help by means of him, and they consider that associating with Him a partner in his Divinity, declaring that His Divinity is too transcendent for that, they at the same time annul this transcendence when they insist on making his "firm establishment on His throne" at once:

- a literal affirmation of the throne,
- a taking up a spatial position with respect to it, and
- being physically situated at a higher level above it.

They further corrupt divine transcendence by making Him a holder of the heavens in one finger, the earth in another, the trees in another, and the angels in yet another. Then, they affirm of Him spatial direction placing Him above the heavens fixed upon the throne so a person can to point to Him in a sensible fashion. Also, they say that he literally descends to the lower heavens and ascends from thence. Accordingly, one of them recites:

"If affirming God's establishment on His throne
means He is body, then I make Him a body!
If affirming His attributes is making Him like something,

then I do not hesitate to make Him like something!
If denying establishment on His throne, or His attributes,
or His speech is to avoid anthropomorphism
Then I deny that our Lord avoids anthropomorphism!
He alone grants success,
and He knows best and is more sublime."

Now I shall relate to you the way at least one of the Wahhabiyya expresses his doctrine in a book entitled "The Pure and Undefiled Religion."[11] The author says that by body one means either what is made up of matter and form according to the philosophers; or what is composed of the atom according to the theologians. All this, he says, is categorically denied of God, the Exalted. But the correct view -- he says -- denies it of contingent[12] beings as well; for neither are the bodies of creatures composed of matter and form nor of atom. Note how far off the beaten track and eccentric his mode of expression is here. For, on the one hand, he claims that in its generally accepted meaning "body" is either a hylomorphic[13] or an atomic compound. On the other hand, he rejects the existence of "body" in this sense whether the body in question be necessary[14] or contingent. Evidently, the purpose of this denial is to arrive at a denial of corporeality. This follows from his own opinion concerning God: since he does not want it said that he likens the Creator to the creature, he denies corporeality to the creature but only in the sense of a hylomorphic or atomic compound, taking it for granted that the reader will be cognizant of the fact no body is made up purely of matter and form -- as the philosophers have it.

But, then, he is left with it being composed of atoms. Yet his ignorance does not lie in the strange claim that "body" possesses

---

[11]Muhammad Siddiq Hasan, Nawab of Bhopal (1832-1890), author of *al-Din al-khalis* in 4 volumes (Cairo: Maktabat dar al-`urubah, 1956-1960).

[12]I.e. created.

[13]I.e. composed of both corporeal and spiritual matter.

[14]I.e. non-created.

no limit at which it ends.[15] It is no wonder that he arrives at this abominable confusion. I wish he had explained, after his denial of body's being a hylomorphic compound, what order of bodily composition he has in mind. I do not think even his muddle-headedness allows him to hold to the claim that bodies are made up of infinitely divisible parts. The ulama of Kalam or dialectical theologians reject this position without exception. Today's science denies it as well. Besides, any demonstrative proof one can produce will vouchsafe its invalidity. To delve into an explanation of why this is so would take us beyond our proper business.

So to return to the present discussion, we note that the Wahhabi author, casting his first definition aside, goes on to say that if one means by body what is characterized by attributes and means by this that bodies see by means of vision, talk, speak, hear, are pleased, are angry, then these are ideas affirmed of the Lord, the Exalted, as well insofar as one ascribes such attributes to Him. Hence, to characterize bodies as seeing, hearing, etc. cannot constitute denial of the same attributes to Him.

I reply: We know of no one who defines body as something which talks, speaks, hears, sees, which is pleased and is angry. These attributes exist only in a living being possessed of intelligence. To be sure, the body sees by means of vision just as he says. But his affirmation of body to God in this sense is to bring Him down to the level of His creatures because of what it simultaneously denies about His Divinity. When predicated of God, being a body in this sense is an imperfection and deficiency which is obligatorily rejected.

As from the standpoint of reason, according to the scientific explanation given in optics, sight is only brought about by the radiation of light on the surface of a visible object and the reflection of light-rays on the organ of vision. Given this, we must first suppose the existence of an object of vision which possesses, as we said, a surface on which light-rays fall. And that, in turn,

---

[15]I.e. it lies in graver conclusions yet.

requires an object made up of parts. But here we take a fall, if our purpose is to characterize Divinity. This is because the body in this sense is identical to the definition of "body" which the Wahhabi author of "The Pure and Undefiled Religion" denies is true of God at the outset. Indeed, he denies that body in this sense applies to any contingent *(mumkin)* being.

From the standpoint of transmitted proof-texts God says: "Sight does not perceive Him yet He perceives sight" (6: 103). There is no conflict of this verse with the verse: "Faces on that day will be bright looking at their Lord" (75: 22). For the mode of this vision of Him on the day of resurrection is unknown just as true doctrine teaches and proclaims. It is possible that vision on that day consists of a kind of uncovering without a need of sight which is, strictly speaking, without parallel. Indeed, the text's use of "faces" signifies precisely that inasmuch as He did not say eyes. And its saying "bright" expresses clearly the occurrence of the perfected attitude experienced by the faces as a result of that unveiling.

Then he says "If you mean by body what can be pointed to in a sensible fashion then the most knowing of God among His creatures pointed to Him by his finger raising it up to the sky,"[16] etc. then I reply that common sense judges that what is pointed to in a sensible way must be in a direction and a place and must be an object of vision -- and all of that is impossible concerning God. If God the Most Exalted were in a direction or a place, then place and direction would exist before He did whereas demonstrable proof exists that there is no priority without beginning other than God. Furthermore, if He were in a place then He would need that place and this would constitute a denial of His absolute self-sufficiency.[17]

---

[16]An aberrant, anthropomorphizing interpretation of the hadith in *Sahih Muslim* (English ed. 2:616) whereby at the end of the Farewell Pilgrimage the Prophet pointed his finger in turn at the sky then at the people, saying: "O Allah, be witness, O Allah, be witness, O Allah, be witness."

[17]In *kalam* or theology God's "necessity" *(wujub)* is a reference to necessary existence and self-sufficiency, which applies to God alone, whereas all other existence possesses only "contingency" *(imkan)*.

Still further, if He were in a place then He would be in it sometimes or at all times. The first alternative is false because moments in time are similar in themselves. Likewise God's relation to moments of time is all the same so His singling out of one of them would be a gratuitous preference of one time over another if there is no external agent who is responsible for tipping the scales; and if there is, then He would be depending on external factors to achieve spatial confinement. The second alternative is also false since from it follows the insertion of spatially confined things into places already occupied by bodies and that is absurd. Also, were it possible to point to him in a sensible fashion then he could be pointed to from every point on the surface of earth and since the earth is circular it follows that God is surrounded by earth from all directions. Otherwise, pointing to him would be impossible. And since He is firmly established on His throne and has taken a position on it just as the Wahhabis claim, then, his throne is surrounded by the seven heavens. Thus, it follows from His coming down to the lower level and His going up from thence, as the Wahhabis say, that His body becomes small when he goes down and gets big when he goes up. Therefore God would be constantly changing from one state to another!

Now the texts from the transmitted sources of Qur'an and Sunna establishing that He can be pointed to and of which the Wahhabis lay hold -- these they understand superficially and they in no wise contradict certainties. They are interpreted *(tu'awwal)* either in a general sense -- and the detailed meanings are left to God himself, just as the majority of the pious ancestors are in agreement on; or they are interpreted in a detailed fashion as according to the opinion of many, in that what is mentioned about pointing him to the heavens is predicated upon the fact that God is the creator of the heavens or that the heavens are the manifestation of His power because of what they contain in the way of the great worlds in relation to which our humble world is only an atom. Likewise ascent to him is in the sense of ascent to the place to which one draws near by acts of obedience and so forth and so on with respect to Qur'anic exegesis.

5: How the Wahhabis Cast Aside Reason Since clear reason and sound theory clash in every way with what the Wahhabis believe, they are forced to cast reason aside. Thus by their taking the text of Qur'an and Sunna only in their apparent meaning *(zahir)* absurdity results. Indeed, this is the well spring of their error and misguidance. For by attending only to the apparent meaning of the Qur'anic text, they believe that God being fixed on His throne and being high above his throne is literally true and that he literally has a face, two hands and that his coming down and his going up is a literal going down and coming up and that he may be pointed to in the sky with the fingers in a sensible manner and so forth. According to this interpretation, God is made into nothing less than a body. These very Wahhabis, who call visiting graves idol-worship, then, become themselves idol-worshippers by fashioning the object they worship into a body, like an animal who sits on its seat and literally comes down and goes up and literally has a hand and a foot and fingers. But the true object of worship, God the Exalted, transcends what they worship.

Still, if one refutes them by rational proofs and establishes that their beliefs contradict the nature of divinity by criteria recognized by reason, they answer that there is no arena for the humble human minds in matters like this whose level is beyond the level of mere reason. In this respect they are exactly like Christians in their claim about the trinity. For ask a Christian: "How is three one and one three?" they will answer: "Knowledge of the Trinity is above reason; it is impermissible to apply reasoning in this area."

There is no doubt that when reason and the transmitted text contradict each other, the transmitted text is interpreted by reason. For often it is impossible for a single judgment to affirm what each of them requires because of what is entailed by the simultaneous holding together of two contradictory propositions. Taking one side or the other, in other words, does not relieve the conflict. On the contrary, one must choose either priority of the transmitted text over reason or reason over the transmitted text. Now the first of these two alternatives has to be invalid simply because it represents the invalidation of the root by the branch.

Clearly, one can affirm the transmitted text only by virtue of reason. That is because affirmation of the Creator, knowledge of prophecy and the rest of the conditions of a transmitted text's soundness are only fulfilled by aid of reason. Thus reason is the principle behind the transmitted text on which its soundness depends. So, if the transmitted text is given precedence over reason and its legal implication established by itself aside from the exercise of reason, then the root would be invalidated by the branch. And from that the invalidation of the branch would follow as well. For the soundness of the transmitted text is derived from the judgment of reason whose corruption is made possible when reason is invalidated.

So reason is not cut off by the soundness of the transmitted text. Hence, it follows that declaring the transmitted text sound by making it prior to reason constitutes nothing less than the voiding of its soundness. But if making something sound accomplishes its corruption we face a contradiction: the transmitted text, then, is invalid. Therefore, if the priority of the transmitted text over reason does not exist on the basis of the preceding argument, then we have determined that reason has priority over the transmitted source. And that is what we set out to prove.

Once one realizes this, one also realizes without question the necessity of interpreting the Qur'anic verses where the apparent sense contradicts reason when the said verses are obscure and do not refer to things that are known with certainty *(yaqinat)*. On the one hand, there is general interpretation where the detailed clarification is left to God *(tafwid tafsilih)*. This is the school of the majority of the Pious Ancestors of our Faith *(al-Salaf)*. On the other hand, we have interpretation which sets out the text's meaning in a more perspicuous fashion. The majority of later scholars *(al-khalaf)* follow the latter. In their view:

- The term "to firmly establish" as in the verse of Qur'an: "The All-Merciful is firmly established on His throne" (20:18) means "He took possession of it" *(istawla)*. This is supported by the words of the poet who said: "`Amr took possession *(qad istawla)* of Iraq without bloodshed or sword."

- God's saying: "And your Lord comes with angels rank on rank" (89:22) means his power comes.[18]
- His saying: "Unto Him good words ascend" (35:10) means: good words please Him.[19] For the word is an accident for which, by itself, locomotion is impossible.
- His saying: "Wait they for naught else than that Allah should come unto them in the shadows of the clouds with the angels?" (2:210) means that His punishment should come unto them.[20]
- His saying: "Then He drew near and came down until he was two bows' length or nearer" (53:8-9) means that the Prophet came near Him by virtue of his obedience. The length of two bow-lengths is a pictorial representation in sensible fashion of what the mind understands.
- In the Prophet's saying in Bukhari and Muslim: "God comes down to the nearest heaven and says: who is repenting, I shall turn to him, and who seeks forgiveness, I shall forgive him" the coming down signifies God's mercy.[21] He specifies night because it is the time of seclusion and various kinds of acts of humility and worship and so forth among verses of Qur'an and narrations of the Prophet.

---

[18]Or His reward, as Imam Ahmad interpreted it. See Bayhaqi's sound report in Ibn Kathir's *al-Bidaya wa al-nihaya* 10:327 and Ibn al-Jawzi's *Daf` shubah al-tashbih* (Saqqaf ed.) p. 13.

[19]Or His acceptance, as interpreted by Abu Hayyan in *Tafsir al-bahr al-muhit* (7:303) and Bayhaqi in Ibn Hajar's *Fath al-Bari* (13:416).

[20]Or: His power and His order, as Imam Ahmad interpreted it. See Bayhaqi's sound report in Ibn Kathir's *al-Bidaya wa al-nihaya* 10:327 and Ibn al-Jawzi's *Daf` shubah al-tashbih* (Saqqaf ed.) p. 110 and 141.

[21]As reported also from some of the Salaf, such as Imam Malik: see Ibn `Abd al-Barr, *al-Tamhid* (7:143) and Dhahabi, *Siyar a`lam al-nubala'* (8:105).

5: Wahhabi Rejection Of Consensus *(Ijma`)*

Since the very substance of the Wahhabi creed contradicts what the noble Companions, the great Mujtahids and the totality of the Ulama have reached a consensus on, they must reject Consensus as a principle *(asl)* of Islamic legislation and deny its probative value as a basis for practical application. In consequence, they have declared disbeliever any Muslim who says "There is no god but God and Muhammad is the Messenger of God" other than themselves because Muslims visit the graves of prophets and awliya, and ask God for something for the sake of a prophet.

They pronounce this declaration of unbelief despite the fact that the Muslim Community has reached a consensus that whoever articulates the twofold testimony of faith or shahada, the ordinances of the religion become immediately binding. As we have seen from the hadith: "I have been ordered to fight people until they say: There is no god but God" and the hadith: "It is sufficient that folk say: There is no God but God is sufficient." Ibn Qayyim has said: "Muslims have reached a consensus that when the disbeliever says : There is no god but God and Muhammad is the Messenger of God, he enters Islam." For that reason, there is a general agreement that when the apostate apostatizes by an act of idolatry, repentance is accomplished by utterance of the shahada.

Furthermore, Wahhabis consider seeking the intercession of the Prophet after his death an act of disbelief *(kufr)* even though a consensus allowing it is in place. At the same time, they say following and emulating the legal rulings of one of the four mujtahids, Imam Abu Hanifa, Imam Shafi`i, Imam Malik and Imam Ahmad Ibn Hanbal is prohibited. As a result, anyone, they say, may derive legal rulings *(istinbat al-ahkam)* directly from the Qur'an according to their capability; notwithstanding the existence of consensus to the effect that no one is capable of being an Imam in the religion or school of law unless he satisfies the criteria for a scholar capable of legal reasoning *(mujtahid)*. It is not up to anyone to take from Qur'an and Sunna until he has satisfied those criteria by joining in himself the qualifications of the *mujtahid* which are, simultaneously, the conditions of *ijithad.*

Ijtihad is the agreement of the mujtahids of the Muslim community in a certain generation on a matter of religion or dogma. A corollary to this is that consensus on any matter is absent after the disappearance of a generation of mujtahids. While this is the case, one knows that if no consensus has been agreed upon, there exists a possibility in each generation of reaching a settlement on questions about which a clear ruling in Qur'an and Sunna is absent and which mujtahids of the past have not discussed.

Consider these examples. A man hears it said that the earth is moving around the sun. Without thinking, he says: "If the earth is moving around the sun, then my wife is divorced," since there is no clear evidence in Qur'an and Sunna for affirming the earth's movement around the sun. The ulama of the Muslim community therefore need to make a clear pronouncement regarding this question. Hence, their consensus regarding the earth's motion does not exist until a question like this is settled.

Or, suppose a man fasts, riding in a balloon in the air before the setting of the sun and he is lifted into the air until he arrived at the height of ten thousand miles. Then the sun sets on earth and the people on land break their fast but the sun is not absent from his eyes when he is in the air by reason of the earth's roundness. Is it permitted for him to break fast and it is obligatory for him to pray salat al-Maghrib? This is an example where there is no clear ruling upon in Qur'an and Sunna. It follows, then, that the ulama of a generation must clarify a judgment of things like this and agree upon it. And what we say agrees with Imam Ghazali's definition of ijma`. He defines it as agreement of the community of Muhammad (s) upon a certain matter and what is meant by agreement is the manifest and unhidden agreement of its ulama.

Those that deny *ijma`* claim: the occurrence of such a consensus is impossible. They deduce evidence for their denial by arguing that agreement of the ulama presupposes their being equally placed with regard to the legal situation in question. Their being scattered in remote countries over the face of the earth precludes this. We refute this objection by rejecting the reasoning that the ulama's being spread abroad is an impediment to their agreement in view of the (unconditional) strictness of their scrutiny of Shari`a evidences.

Those rejecting ijma` claim further that agreement is based either on an indication *(dalil)* in the sources which is decisive *(qat'i)* or on a speculative one *(zanni)*. Both, they say, are invalid. The decisive indication is invalid because, they say, if it were existent there would be no need for recourse to agreement in the first place; and the speculative indication is invalid because agreement on a ruling is impossible since temperaments differ and points of view differ out of natural habit. Our answer is a rejection of both their objections. Regarding the decisive indication there is no need of transmitting it since consensus is stronger than it, and for the elimination of difference entailed through its transmission. With regard to the speculative indication, their objection does not stand up because of the possibility of consensus being too obvious for either differences of temperament and/or point of view to prevent it. Only in what is minute and obscure lie impediments to reaching consensus.

In further objection, they claim: Even if we grant establishment of consensus in itself, then knowledge of their agreement would still be impossible. They argue that in the habitual course of things there is no chance of affirmation of a legal ruling concerning this thing or the other declared by every individual member of the ulama in the world. Likewise, they argue that in the habitual course of things transmission of a consensus is impossible because its transmission from single individuals is not conveyed and the consensus does not issue in practical application. One simply cannot conceive of a thing being so widely known that lying about it is impossible *(tawatur)* -- they claim -- inasmuch as such a situation would involve the necessary equaling out of points of view on a given state of affairs with the result that pro and con positions and a middle position would be unfeasible. Moreover, it is unlikely that people informed of something so well-known that lying about it is impossible to have seen and heard all the ulama in every country and in that fashion to have transmitted it from them, generation to generation, until it reaches us.

To both their arguments there is one answer. Its procedure consists in causing one to doubt that there exists a conflict with what is necessary. For it is well known in a decisive manner that the Companions and the Successors reached a consensus on the priority of a decisive indication over a speculative one and that this is the case only by reason of its being established with them and its transmission to us. Furthermore, ijma` constitutes a proof in the view of all the ulama except the Mu'tazilite al-Nazzam and some of the Khawarij. The proof of its evidentiary nature *(hujjiyya)* is that they agree upon the decisive certainty of the error of contradicting ijma`. Ijma` therefore counts as proof in Shari`a legislation because custom transforms the agreement of a number of many recognized ulama from the status of non-decisive to the status of decisive certainty in a matter pertaining to the Shari`a. By virtue of custom the implication of a decisive text necessarily counts as decisive indication that to contradict ijma` is error.

On this point, no one says here that there is affirmation of ijma` by ijma` nor affirmation of ijma` by a decisive text whose establishment is itself dependent on ijma`: that would be to reason in a circle. We are saying: what is being claimed is that the fact of ijma` itself constitutes a proof for ijma`. What establishes this is the existence of a decisive text indicated by the existence of a formal consensus, which custom precludes were it not for that text. The establishment of this formal consensus and its customary indications pointing to the existence of a text are not dependent upon the fact that ijma` constitutes a proof. This is because the existence of such formal consensus is derived from *tawatur* -- what is known as true beyond doubt so that the possibility of people's collusion on a lie is precluded -- and because the formal evidence indicating a text is derived from the custom.

Among the evidences for the probative value of ijma` is the Prophet's statement, on him be peace:

"My community will never agree on error *(al-khata')*."

The content of this hadith is so well-known that it is impossible to lie about it *(mutawatir)*[22] simply because it is produced in so many narrations, for example:

"My community will not come together on a misguidance";[23]

"A group of my community will continue in truth until the dawning of the Hour";[24]

"The hand of God is with the congregation *(al-jama`a)*";[25]

"Whoever leaves the community or separates himself from it by the length of a span, dies the death of the Jahiliyya (period of ignorance prior to Islam)";[26]

---

[22]"Ghazali has pointed out that this hadith is not *mutawatir*... Having said this, however, al-Ghazali adds [*Mustasfa* 1:111] that a number of prominent Companions have reported *ahadith* from the Prophet, which although different on their wording, are all in consonance on the theme of the infallibility of the community and its immunity from error... [Both he and al-Amidi in *al-Ihkam* 1:220-221] observe that the main purport of these *ahadith*... convey positive [*qat`i*] knowledge, and that the infallibility of the *ummah* is sustained by their collective weight." Mohammad Hashim Kamali, *Principles of Islamic Jurisprudence* (Cambridge: Islamic Texts Society, 1991) p. 178. See Ibn al-`Arabi al-Maliki's list of the ahadith pertaining to ijma` in his commentary on Tirmidhi's relevant section in Kitab al-fitan: *`Aridat al-ahwadhi* (Beirut: Dar al-kutub al-`ilmmiyya, n.d.) 9:8-11.

[23]Ibn Majah 2:1303 #3950.

[24]*Mutawatir* (Bukhari and Muslim).

[25]Tirmidhi (hasan).

[26]Muslim (Imara #55) through Ibn `Abbas. Muslim relates it with slight variations through three more chains. Ibn Abi Shayba also relates it in his *Musannaf*.

and so forth. As for the solitary hadiths *(ahad)* involved, even if they are not widely attested, they possess value equivalent to the widely attested hadith and, indeed, positive knowledge results from them just like stories we hear relating the courage of Imam `Ali and the generosity of Hatim.

The deniers of the evidentiary nature of ijma` use as proof the verse from the Qur'an: "And We reveal the Scripture unto thee as an exposition of all things" (16:89). Then they say that there is no reference for the exposition of legal rulings except the Qur'an. The answer to them is this does not preclude that there can be something other than the Book also exposing matters; nor does it preclude that the Book can expose certain things by means of the ijma`. If it did, we would wind up with external meanings which nevertheless do not oppose the decisive texts.[27]

They also invoke against the probative nature of ijma` God's statement: "If you differ in anything among yourselves, refer it to God and His Messenger" (4:59). Therefore there is no source of reference, they claim, other than Qur'an and Sunna. The answer is: this text refers specifically to what people are "differing about." But what is agreed upon is not like that. Or it specifically concerns the Companions. If we were to accept that this is not the case, then, again, one ends up with external meanings not clashing with what is decisive just as we claimed earlier.

In addition, they adduced the hadith of Mu`adh as evidence that he left out ijma` when he mentioned his evidences in answer to the Prophet's query about them, and the Prophet approved what he said.[28] They say this indicates that ijma` does not count as

---

[27]*Al-zahir la yuqawimu al-qati`*: "The external sense does not stand in opposition to what is decisively known.

[28]It is reported that the Prophet asked Mu`adh ibn Jabal upon the latter's departure as judge to the Yemen: "How will you apply judgment when the occasion arises?" He said: "I shall judge according to Allah's Book." The Prophet asked: "And if you do not find [an answer]?" He said: "Then by the Sunna of His Messenger." The Prophet said: "And if you do not find [an answer]?" He said: "Then I shall do my

evidence. The answer is Mu`adh did not mention it only because at that time ijma` did not yet constitute a formal proof in case of failing to settle upon a source with respect to Qur'an and Sunna. It does not follow that ijma` did not become a proof in its own good time and after taking its place as a source.

6: The Wahhabis' Denial of the Principle of Analogy *(Qiyas)*

Wahhabis reject analogy *(qiyas)* in legal reasoning just as they reject consensus. By rejecting it, however, they only intend to discredit the authority of those truly capable of independent reasoning in deriving legal rulings in the Muslim Community, that is, the mujtahids of the four recognized schools of Islamic law. The Wahhabis allege that the mujtahids cast aside the Qur'an and Sunna and operate only on the basis of their personal opinions to the point of criticizing the Imams of the Umma for using qiyas as a proof in Shari`a. They denounce by saying that the Imams believe that the religion of Islam is deficient and that they complete it by reasoning like of ijma` and qiyas. For this, they cite the Qur'anic verse: "This day I have perfected for you your religion" (5:3). They say we find whatever is necessary for life clearly stated in the Qur'an. So what need do we have for qiyas. The texts take in the whole of life's eventualities, they claim, without need of derivation *(istinbat)* and analogy.

It is amazing that the Wahhabis, for the sake of calumny against mujtahids who accept qiyas themselves, proceed to toy with the word of God and verses of Qur'an and manipulate them, changing them from their correct meaning and interpreting them according to their own passion and whim. And yet they have no interpretation of the superficial sense of the verses of the Qur'an that does not disparage the Creator -- in keeping with their

---

best to form an opinion and spare no pain." The prophet slapped his chest and said: "Praise belongs to God Who has blessed the messenger of God's Messenger's with something pleasing to God's Messenger." Related by Abu Dawud (Eng. 3:1019 #3585).

literalism according to which God is established firmly on His throne and has hands and a face. They say that the mujtahids operate according to their own opinions, even though they go so far as to allow the ignorant riffraff of those possessing their faith to comment upon the Word of God according to their own limited understanding.

Qiyas is the equating of the branch with the root with respect to the cause of the legal ruling. Its essential elements are four:

(1) the original root which is the object of comparison;
(2) the branch or subsidiary case being likened to root;
(3) the ruling governing the root;
(4) the general attribute which is the aspect under which the comparison is being made.

The legal ruling of the new case is not an essential element of it since it is the fruit of the analogy and its consequence. An example of analogy is when we say a drink made of fermented figs is an intoxicant, then it is forbidden by analogy to wine by the evidence of the statement: "Wine is prohibited":[29]

(1) The original case is wine, that is, the object of comparison.
(2) The new case which is like it is the drink made from fermented figs which is what is being compared to the wine.
(3) The legal ruling in the original case is prohibition.
(4) The general attribute is intoxication.

Analogy counts as a proof because the Companions had acted by it repeatedly despite the silence of the others. In a case like that the silence is the agreement of custom because of Qur'anic command: *fa`tabiru* -- "Consider and reflect!" (59:2). It is well known that "consideration" consists of making an analogy of one thing to another which is not an exception.

---

[29] Anas and others in Bukhari and Muslim.

Even if this did not constitute an argument, many matters would remain that we see come into existence in the course of time whose legal status is overlooked, and regarding whose status the criteria for judging are absent from the apparent meaning of the texts in the Qur'an and Sunna. Yet this does not contradict God's statement: "There is not a grain in the darkness or depths of the earth, nor anything fresh or dry but is inscribed in a clear Record" (6:59). What is meant by "clear Record" here is the Preserved Tablet on which God has deposited what was and what will be.

We may say that since the root of the analogy is mentioned with its legal ruling in the Book, the branch to which the root's ruling is applied is considered mentioned as well, for it is built upon the root. Or again we say: It is obvious that the manner in which the content of the Book of God embraces every green and dry is not all explicit. Rather, many of the legal rulings of Qur'an come into being by pure derivation *(istinbatan)*. And among the modes of derivation there is qiyas. So the Wahhabis' statement whereby the texts of Qur'an and hadith pertain to all of life's phenomena without derivation or analogy is not granted. Their containing all of life's phenomena is only complete by their application.

7: Their Denial of *Taqlid* and of the *Ijtihad* of Past Sunni Scholars

Since the statements of the Mujtahids of the past -- may God have mercy upon them -- and the established religious rulings to which they have arrived clash with what the deviant sect of Wahhabis have devised in the way of unwarranted innovation, that sect deemed it a necessity to deny the validity of their ijtihad, reject the soundness of their opinions, and declare whoever followed their opinions to be an unbeliever. The result of this is that they have the freedom of action to establish themselves far and wide and to scream and play with the religion just as their passions dictate. Thus, they pave the way for founding the basis of their clear misguidance. For if they did not deny the ijtihad of the Mujtahids of the past, then their application, in accordance with their whim, of the verses of the Qur'an revealed concerning idolaters to Muslims and to those who make their petitions to God for the sake of the honor of His Messenger and respect of the saints *(awliya)* could not have been brought to pass. That is because they focus on what no Mujtahid said in the first place and what none of Imams of the Religion accepted.

All of this misguidance is due to the unwarranted innovator Ibn `Abd al-Wahhab who displayed marked resemblance to those who claimed prophethood like Musaylima and Abu al-Aswad al-Anasi and other liars. For he was concealing in himself the establishment of a religion which imitated the pattern of those liars. But he feared to show people his lies unlike they who showed their lies. What he made appear to people he put in the guise of support of the Islamic faith while he painted this picture in people's minds that he simply wanted pure monotheism and that people had become idolaters. Thus, the jihad with people followed so that they might "return from their idolatry." Therefore, Ibn `Abd al-Wahhab claimed absolute ijtihad for himself and charged with error whoever preceded him belonging to the Mujtahids -- those great figures who dipped from the sea of knowledge of the Prophet -- and declared disbeliever their followers. He did not permit imitating the opinions of anyone other than himself, although he allowed anyone his of his ignorant followers to interpret the Qur'an in whatever mode their limited understanding gave them access, and to derive legal rulings from them on the basis of their weak grasp of its meaning. It was as though he permitted any one of his followers to be a mujtahid. Look at the way he played with religion and toyed with the Shari`a of the Faithful Messenger of God!

As for his claim of absolute ijtihad, it is pure silliness on his part and shameless impudence with regard to the Arab language since he was not in his time one of those recognized for being foremost in knowledge. On the contrary, he was not even numbered among those who were considered by masters in the Hanbali madhhab as having any weight whatsoever, not to mention being considered an absolute mujtahid in the religion.

Ijtihad has conditions which the ulama have agreed upon without exception and it is not permissible for any individual to be an imam in the religion and in any of the schools of Islamic Law, unless he has fulfilled them.

Conditions of Ijtihad (1) He must be a master of the language of the Arabs, knowing its different dialects, the import of their poems, their proverbs, and their customs.[30]

(2) He must have a complete grasp of the differing opinions of the scholars and jurists of Islam.[31]

(3) He must be a jurist himself, learned in the Qur'an, having memorized it and knowing the difference of the seven readings of the Qur'an while understanding its commentary, being aware of what is clear and what is obscure in it, what it abrogates and what is abrogated by it, and the stories of the prophets.

(4) He must be learned in the Sunna of the Messenger of God, capable of distinguishing between its sound hadith and its weak hadith, its continuous hadith and hadith whose chain of transmission is broken, its chains of transmission, as well as those hadith which are well known.[32]

(5) He must be scrupulously pious in the religion, restraining his lower desires with respect to righteousness and trustworthiness, and his doctrine must be built upon the Qur'an and the Sunna of the Prophet. One who is missing in any of these characteristics falls short and is not permitted to be a Mujtahid whom people imitate.[33]

---

[30]It is not necessary, according to consensus, that he possess profound erudition in the Arabic language *(tabahhur)*, but it is enough that he have a moderate erudition *(tawassut)* as described by Zahawi.

[31]By this are meant the science of differences of opinions *(`ilm al-khilaf)*, the science of consensus in opinions *(`ilm al-ijma`)*, and the science of analogy and its kinds *(`ilm al-qiyas)*.

[32]It is not necessary that he reach the rank of hadith master *(hafiz)*, as Suyuti in *al-radd `ala man akhlad* points out by listing non-hafiz absolute mujtahids *(mujtahid mutlaq)* such as Abu Ishaq al-Shirazi, Ibn al-Sabbagh, al-Juwayni, and al-Ghazali.

[33]Suyuti has listed among the mujtahids whose mastership is recognized at one and the same time in the three fields of jurisprudence,

Ibn al-Qayyim in *I'lam al-muwaqqi'in* does not permit anyone to make derivation from the Qur'an and Sunna as long as he has not fulfilled the conditions of ijtihad with respect to the Islamic sciences. A man asked Ahmad Ibn Hanbal: "If a person memorized a hundred thousand hadiths, is he a jurist *(faqih)*?" Imam Ahmad said: "No." He said: "Two hundred thousand hadiths?" Imam Ahmad said: "No." Three hundred thousand hadiths? Again, he said: "No." "Four hundred thousand hadiths?" Finally, he said: "Yes."[34] It is said that Ahmad Ibn Hanbal gave legal answers on the basis of six hundred thousand hadith.[35]

Know that people have agreed generation after generation and century after century that the Mujtahid Imams only derive legal rulings from the Qur'an and the Sunna after they have completely studied the Sunna and its sciences and the Qur'an with respect to its rulings and understanding, in a way unmatched by those who followed them in later times. On the contrary, the ulama, generation after generation, take hold of what they said , scholars of the caliber of al-Nawawi, al-Rafi'i, Taqi al-Din al-Subki, Ibn Hazm, Ibn Taymiyya, Ibn al-Qayyim, Ibn al-Jawzi, scholars like Fakhr al-Din al-Razi, al-Tahawi, al-Qasim, al-Qarafi: all were imitating the opinions of the Mujtahids and their followers, despite the fact that each one of these leading figures and those before them had delved deep into every category of the Islamic sciences. Yet and still, they knew that they had not arrived at the level of deriving law

---

hadith, and the Arabic language: himself, Ibn al-Salah, Abu Shama, al-Nawawi, Ibn Daqiq al-'Id, and Taqi al-Din al-Subki among others.

[34]Al-Sakhawi relates in the introduction to his biography of Ibn Hajar al-'Asqalani entitled *al-Jawahir wa al-durar* that Ahmad said neither yes nor no to the figure of 300,000, but he gestured with his hand that it was acceptable (Cairo 1986 ed. p. 26). Ibn al-Jawzi relates in *al-Hathth 'ala hafz al-'ilm* (Alexandria ed. 1983 p. 43) that Abu Zur'a said that Imam Ahmad knew no less than 1,000,000 hadiths.

[35]According to Imam Ahmad's statement reported by Al-Hakim in his *Madkhal li 'ulum al-hadith* (Robson ed. p. 13) there were 7,000,000 sound hadiths known in his time, of which the hafiz Abu Zur'a had memorized 6; and he sat at Bukhari's feet like a young boy learning. All these numbers refer to chains of transmission, not texts.

from Qur'an and Sunna independently. What's more, they understood their own limits. May God have mercy on the man who knows his measure and does not go beyond his proper level.

So how is it possible for any one of us from this later time to derive law from Qur'an and Sunna and to cast aside the ulama who were capable of deriving law and whom both the elite and the masses of the Muslims agree on following?

Ibn `Abd al-Wahhab's labeling disbeliever those who imitate the opinion of the Mujtahids of the past, as mentioned previously is only to initiate spread of his unwarranted innovation *(bid`a)* in our faith so that he may only considers Muslim those who follow him. Would that I knew what would happen if we supposed that past Mujtahids had gone astray, as Ibn `Abd al-Wahhab has claimed, and they had, indeed, gone astray. Would it be incumbent upon the common person to practice Islam while being unable to know how to derive legal rulings from Qur'an and Sunna with Ibn `Abd al-Wahhab having not yet been born to resolve the difficulty of their confusion and ignorance? I do not believe that he would have arrived at the temerity to say those people were living in the primordial state of natural religion *(fitra)* since they came in a time prior to a "renewer of religion"![36]

---

[36]These are the renewers of religion according to Ahl al-Sunna:
1st Century: `Umar ibn `Abd al-Aziz (62-101)
2nd: Abu Hanifa (80-150), Malik (93-179), al-Shafi`i (150-204)
3rd: Ahmad ibn Hanbal (164-241), Abu al-Hasan al-Ash'ari (260-324)
4th: al-Hakim al-Naysaburi (321-405)
5th: al-Bayhaqi (384-458), al-Ghazali (450-505)
6th: Fakhr al-din al-Razi (544-606)
7th: al-Nawawi (631-676), Ibn Daqiq al-`Eid (?-702)
8th: Taqi al-Din al-Subki (683-756), al-Bulqini (724-805)
9th: al-`Asqalani (773-852), al-Suyuti (849-911)
10th: al-Sha`rani (898-973)
11th: al-Faruqi al-Sirhindi (971-1034)
12th: Ibn `Alawi al-Haddad (1046-1132)
13th: Khalid al-Baghdadi (1193-1242)
14th: al-Kawthari (d. 1371)

The present writer knows that following an authority in matter of Islamic practice *(al-taqlid)* is necessary inasmuch as, ordinarily speaking, it is impossible that each individual Muslim reach the level of knowledge enabling him to derive legal rulings of the Shari`a directly from Qur'an when there is no plain meaning text and he is completely ignorant of the Arabic language like non-Arab people such as Persians, Kurd, Afghans, Turks, and others whose number increases beyond the number of Arabs, a fact obvious to any one with a knowledge of geography. The scholars of Islam have agreed that it is incumbent upon a person who has not reached the stage of ijtihad to follow and imitate the legal rulings of a mujtahid. For God has said: "Ask those who have knowledge *(Ahl al-dhikr)* if you do not know." (16: 43) and the Prophet said, on him be peace: "Did they ask when they did not know? For the only remedy of incapacity in such instances is to ask a question."[37]

8: Their Naming Muslims Disbelievers *(Takfir)*

Wahhabis have pretexts for their doctrine to in order to construct a foundation for their unwarranted innovation in religion. One of them is to declare Muslims unbelievers. That is because Ibn `Abd al-Wahhab, as you know by now, has been seduced by the evil promptings of his ego into attempting to create a new religion by which he could obtain political leadership. However, when he saw that this could not be brought to pass in the land of Muslims -- for, in spite of their

---

[37]Related by Abu Dawud.

Ibn Qayyim said: "There is an obligatory (wajib) taqlid, a forbidden taqlid, and a permitted taqlid... The obligatory taqlid is the taqlid of those who know better than us, as when a person has not obtained knowledge of an evidence from the Qur'an or the Sunna concerning something. Such a taqlid has been reported from Imam al-Shafi`i in many places, where he would say: "I said this in taqlid of `Umar" or "I said that in taqlid of `Uthman" or "I said that in taqlid of `Ata'." As Al-Shafi`i said concerning the Companions -- may God be well pleased with all of them: "Their opinion for us is better than our opinion to ourselves."" Ibn Qayyim, *A`lam al-muwaqqi`in `an rabb al-`alamin* 2:186-187.

extreme ignorance, they held fast to the faith of Islam -- he created the innovation in Islam itself. Furthermore, when he saw that the matter could not be accomplished except after declaring Muslims disbelievers by using some semblance of Qur'anic evidence, he found that the only way to declare them unbelievers was through their calling on God by using their Prophet as a means *(tawassul)* as well as for the sakes of other prophets, awliya and pious persons. Likewise he levelled the same charge at those who vow or perform sacrifices for their sakes and perform other acts whose description I shall bring later. All these matters he considers worship of the Prophets and the saints. And since the Qur'an is jam-packed with clearly articulated verses to the effect that one who worships something or someone other than God, he is an idolater, Ibn `Abd al-Wahhab makes all monotheists idolaters because of the state of affairs just described.

Since the Wahhabis have declared disbeliever all Muslims who differ with them, they have made their country the land of warfare *(bilad harb)*. Then they have made licit the shedding their blood and seizing their property. Yet God, the Exalted, has said: "Surely, religion with God is the Surrender *(al-Islam)*" (3:19). And the Prophet has said: "Islam consists in testifying that there is no god but God and that Muhammad is the Messenger of God." Also, in the hadith of Ibn `Umar we find: " Islam is built upon five things: Testifying that there is no god but God and that Muhammad is the His servant and Messenger," to the end of the hadith. There is the hadith of the delegation of `Abd al-Qays: "I order you to believe in God alone. Do you know what belief in God alone is? It is to bear witness that there is no god but God and that Muhammad is the Messenger of God."[38] Ibn Qayyim said: "All Muslims agree that if the disbeliever says: There is no god but God and Muhammad is the Messenger of God, he enters Islam."

---

[38] All three are related by Bukhari and Muslim.

Know that to declare a Muslim a unbeliever is no small matter. The ulama, among them Ibn Taymiyya and Ibn Qayyim,[39] have agreed that the ignorant person and the one who makes a mistake in this community, even if what is done makes its perpetrator an idolater or disbeliever, and that person pleads the excuse of ignorance or that he made a mistake until a proof is explained to him in a lucid and clear fashion, a situation like such a person's is ambiguous.[40] The Muslim might have joined in him disbelief, idolatry and faith. Yet he does not disbelieve in such a way that carries him out of the religion.

Apostasies and Heresies The Khawarij were the first to separate from the Congregation of Muslims. The Messenger of God had spoken about them and ordered them to be killed and fought: "They will pass through Islam like an arrow passes through its quarry. Wherever you meet them, kill them!"[41] "They are the dogs of the people in Hell."[42] "They recite Qur'an and consider it in their favor but it is against them."[43] The Khawarij went out of Islam in the time of our master `Ali, may God be pleased with him. They declared him and Mu`awiya disbelievers and declared licit their blood and property as well as the blood and property of those with him. They made the land of the former a land of war and declared their own land an abode of faith. They only accepted from the Prophet's Sunna what agreed with their own doctrine, deduced evidence for their doctrine from what was not perspicuous in the Qur'an, and applied the verses revealed concerning the idolaters to the people of Islam. Yet despite their disbelief, neither the Companions nor the Successors

---

[39]Zahawi mentions them often because Salafis consider them their highest scholarly authorities. Yet, as he shows, they contradict them on many foundational issues, such as this one.

[40]I.e. he cannot be declared an unbeliever.

[41]Bukhari and Muslim have more than one form of this hadith.

[42]Sound (sahih) hadith related through various chains by Ibn Majah, Muqaddima 12, and Ahmad 4:355, 382, 5:250, 253, 256, 269.

[43]These and many other ahadith have been understood by some scholars to apply to the Wahhabis as well. See above, section following the bibliography.

declared them disbelievers, just as Ibn Taymiyya has transmitted. `Ali said to them: "We do not start out killing you nor are you kept out of the mosques of God in which you mention His name. We do not rescind the rights of protection with respect to your life and property afforded you by Islam as long as your hand is with us." The great among the Companions debated the Khawarij, like Ibn `Abbas, until four thousand returned to the truth.

As for the fighting of the people of the *Ridda* -- apostates -- one category among them apostatized Islam and returned to the disbelief which they were on with respect to idol worship. Another category apostatized and followed Musaylima and they were the Banu Hanifa and some other tribes. Yet another group apostatized, followed and agreed with Aswad al-`Anasi in Yemen. Others said claims of Tulayha al-Asadi were true; they were the Ghatafan, Fazara and other tribes. Still others did the same with respect to Sujah. All these denied the prophethood of Muhammad, may God bless him and grant him peace. They refused to pay the tax on Muslims and to pray, abandoning the rest of the Shari`a as well. One class of apostates distinguished between prayer and the tax. They denied the obligatoriness of conveying the latter to the Imam. In reality, those are the People of Rebellion *(baghi)*. The name "Ridda" was attached to them only because of their entry into the throng of the apostates.

The Qadariyya separated from the Congregation of Muslims in the final period of the time of the Companions. They were composed of two sects. The first directly denied the divine Decree *(qadar)*. They said that God did not foreordain His servants to commit acts of disobedience nor does he guide the one in error and foreordain the guidance. In their view, the Muslim is one who makes himself Muslim by himself and the one who prays makes himself a prayer by himself, and so forth and so on with respect to other acts of obedience and disobedience. This sect makes the servant the creator *(khaliq)* of his own deeds instead of God.

The second sect is just the opposite of the first. They claim that God compels people to act in a certain way and that disbelief and disobedience among human creatures are like the black and white color of their skins. In their view, the creature has no part to play in doing none of this. On the contrary, all acts of disobedience in their view are ascribable to God. The perpetrators of such acts are the followers of Iblis where he says: "Because You have sent me astray, I shall ambush them" (7:16). Similarly, the idolaters say: "Had God willed, we nor our forefathers would not have been idolaters" (6:148). Yet for all this disbelief and misguidance on the part of the Qadariyya, not one of the Companions nor any of the Successors declared them to be disbelievers. Rather, they stood right before them and explained to them their misguidance from the Qur'an and Sunna. They did not make killing them an obligation incumbent on Muslims nor exact against them the judgments made against the people of apostasy.

Then, the Mu`tazila separated from the Congregation of Muslims in the period of the Successors. Among their doctrines of disbelief is their claim that the Qur'an is created. They also deny that the Prophet, on him be God's blessing and peace, can intercede in the behalf of perpetrators of acts of disobedience and assert that perpetrators of disobedience will reside eternally in hell fire and so on and so forth with respect to their teachings. Again, not one of the ulama of that time declared them unbelievers but the scholars among the Successors and those who succeeded them confronted them. They refuted them and explained to them the falsity of their doctrine. They did not exact on them the laws against apostates. On the contrary, on them and those before who made unwarranted innovations in the religion they carried out the Muslim laws of inheritance and marriage and buried them in Muslim ground.

Then there was the Murji'a who claimed that faith *(iman)* resided in the verbal assertion of belief and not in the deed. Hence, in their view, one who articulates the twofold declaration bearing witness to his faith is a believer even if he does not perform a single act of prayer the whole of his life, nor fast one day of Ramadan. Yet despite their lingering in error and their continual dogged resistance to change even after the people of truth explained to them the error of their school of thought, no one declared them unbelievers. Rather, they treated them and the people of unwarranted innovation before them as brethren of fixed and stable faith.

The Jahmiyya separated from the Congregation of Muslims. They said no God who is an object of worship is upon the throne nor does God have any speech as on earth. They denied God the attributes that He affirms of Himself in His clear Book and which His true and faithful Messenger affirms of Him and all the Companions. Likewise, they denied the vision of God in the hereafter and so forth and so on with respect to their doctrines of disbelief. In spite of that, the ulama refuted them and demonstrated to them their misguidance until they killed some of their propagandists like Jahm Ibn Safwan and al-Ju`d Ibn Dirham. But after killing them they ritually cleansed their bodies, prayed for them and buried them in Muslim ground. They did not carry out the rulings for people guilty of apostasy.

Then the Rafida or "Rejecters" separated from the Congregation of Muslims. They agreed with the Mu`tazila in their belief that they were the sole creators of their own actions. They denied the vision of the Creator on the Day of Judgment. They declared most of the Companions to be unbelievers and they vilified the Mother of the Believers (`A'isha). Despite all this non of the `ulama declared them to be unbelievers nor did they forbid the rulings of inheritance and marriage apply to them; rather they applied to them the same rulings that applied with all Muslims.

Those following the school of thought of the Pious Ancestors -- which the Wahhabis attempt to hide behind -- are distinguished by the signal absence of declaring deviant groups unbelievers as we have mentioned. Shaykh Taqi al-Din Ibn Taymiyya said that Imam Ahmad did not declare the Khawarij disbeliever, nor the Murji'a nor the Qadariyya nor the individuals of the Jahmiyya. Indeed, he prayed behind the Jahmiyya who called people to their doctrine while they punished harshly those who did not agree with them. Ibn Taymiyya also said in essence that among the blameworthy innovations is declaring a group among the Muslims to be unbelievers, making their blood and wealth licit because of rejected innovations. For, he said, there may be in that group less unwarranted innovation than in the party carrying out the declaration of disbelief. Even if one supposes a group to have made unwarranted innovation, it is unwarranted for the group which is on the path of the Sunna to declare them unbelievers, since, perhaps, its innovation is an outgrowth of an error, and God said: "Our Lord do not blame us if we forget or make a mistake" (2:286) and: "The mistake you make will not be held against you but what your hearts on purpose intend" (33:5). The Prophet said: "Surely, has God forgiven my community error and forgetfulness and what they were forced to do."[44]

The Consensus has long since concluded that whoever confirms what the Messenger has brought -- even if there be in it some trace of disbelief and idolatry -- should not be declared a unbeliever until the proof is furnished. The only proof that can be furnished is in the strength of Consensus not speculative but decisive. Further, the one who furnishes the proof is the Leader of the Muslims or his deputy. But disbelief only exists when one denies things necessary to the religion of Islam such as the existence of the Creator and his unity, the rejection of the message of Muhammad or the rejection of the duties of Islam like the obligatoriness of prayer.

The school *(madhhab)* of the People of the Prophet's Way and the Congregation of Muslims *(Ahl al-Sunna wa al-Jama`a)* shrinks from declaring anyone belonging to the religion of Islam an unbeliever. This holds even to the point of suspending pronouncements of disbelief against people who introduce unwarranted innovations into Islam, despite the command to kill them out of defense against the harms they may do -- not because of their disbelief. For there may be found joined in a single

---

[44]Ibn Majah, Talaq 16. Tabarani also relates it through two good chains. See Haythami, *Majma` al-zawa'id*.

individual disbelief *(kufr)*, belief *(iman)*, hypocrisy *(nifaq)*, and idolatry *(shirk)* and he is not a complete disbeliever. Whoever confesses Islam it is accepted from him whether he be truthful or lying. Even if signs of hypocrisy and ignorance are manifest on him, he is excused from disbelief. The same is true of hesitation and doubt even if this be weak. By now the unwarranted innovation on the part of the Wahhabis should be manifest in any case, when they introduce an unwarranted innovation by declaring Muslims disbelievers and thereby contradict what God has brought to us in the Qur'an and by the Sunna of His Messenger as well as the statements of the Imams of the religion and the learned mujtahids.

9: The Wahhabis' Rejection of *Tawassul* (Using a means)

In the preceding sections we have spoken about the way the Wahhabis declare any Muslim a disbeliever for contradicting their unwarranted innovations in our religion, and the way they ascribe to that person idolatry. The moment has now come to speak of how they take, as a pretext for their declaration of disbelief, the seeking of help from the prophets and awliya and their use of the latter as a means to God and the visiting of their graves. For the Wahhabis have rejected these practices and claimed they are forbidden *(haram)*.

Their Hatred of Muslims Who Make Tawassul

The Wahhabis have made their rejection of those seeking aid *(mustaghithin)*, those using persons as means of access to God *(mutawassilin)*, and those visiting graves *(za'irin)*, especially intense. They consider them actual idolaters and idol-worshippers. Indeed, they deem their status worse than the idolaters of old. The latter, they say, were idolaters only with respect to divinity. As for the Muslim idolaters -- they mean those who contradict them -- they have associated a partner both to divinity and to lordship. They also say that the unbelievers in the time of the Messenger of God did not always practice idolatry but they sometimes practiced polytheism and sometimes practiced monotheism, abandoning calling on prophets and men of righteousness. That is because when times were good they prayed to them and believed in them. But when disaster and difficulties struck, they abandoned them, worshipped God faithfully and sincerely, and recognized that the prophets and pious could do them neither good nor ill.

Their Assimilation of Muslims to Idol-Worshippers by quoting the Qur'an

The Wahhabis applied the Qur'anic verses revealed concerning the idolaters to the monotheists of the Community of Muhammad, peace be upon him, and grasped on to these verses as a basis for declaring Muslims disbeliever. They may be listed as follows:

- "Do not call on anyone along with God" (72:18);

- "And who is more astray than one who invokes besides God such as will not answer him to the day of judgment and when mankind are gathered they will become enemies for them, and deny having been worshipped" (46:5-6);

- "Nor call on any other than God such as can neither profit thee nor hurt thee: if thou dost, behold! thou shalt certainly be of those who do wrong" (10:106);

- "And those whom you invoke besides Him own not a straw. If ye invoke them, they will not listen to your call, and if they were to listen, they cannot answer your prayer. On the day of Judgment they will reject your partnership and none, O Man! can inform you like Him who is All-aware" (35:13-14);

- "So call not on any other god with God, or thou will be among those who will be punished" (26: 213);

- "To Him is due true prayer; any others that they call upon besides Him hear them no more than if they were to stretch forth their hands for water to reach their mouths but it reaches them not. For the prayer of those without faith is vain prayer" (13:14);

- "Say: Call on those besides Him whom ye fancy; they have no power to remove your trouble from you or to change them. Those unto whom they cry seek for themselves the means of approach to their Lord, which of them shall be the nearest; they hope for His mercy and fear His wrath: for the wrath of thy Lord is something to take heed of" (17:57).

These and other verses have been revealed with respect to the idolaters among the Arabs. Ibn `Abd al-Wahhab, however, claims that whoever seeks help by the Prophet, implores or calls upon God by means of the Prophet of someone else among the prophets, awliya or pious, or asks for the Prophet's intercession or visits his grave is considered in the class of idolaters contained within the scope of the above verses. His specious argument concerning these verses is based on the idea that though they were revealed concerning the idolaters their admonition belongs to the general sense of the expression and not the specificity of the cause.

Refutation of This Falsehood We do not deny that the admonition belongs to the general sense of the expression and not with a specific cause. However, we say that these verses do not refer to the people whom the Wahhabis claim they embrace since the Muslims who make *tawassul* (using means) and *istighatha* (seeking aid) in no way share the state of the unbelievers concerning whom the verses were revealed. Invocation *(du`a)* comes in a variety of senses which we will soon mention. However, in all these verses it has the sense of worship, and Muslims only worship God the Exalted; none of them ever adopted prophets and awliya as gods, making them partners with God so that the general sense of these verses would apply to them. Muslims do not believe that prophets and awliya are entitled to worship since they have not created anything nor do they have control over harm and benefit. On the contrary, they believe that they are God's servants created by Him. By visiting their graves and imploring God in their name they only intend being blessed by means of their blessing for they are alive, near to God and He has selected and chosen them. Hence, he shows mercy to His servants by means of their blessing and heavenly benediction *(baraka)*.

Further False Comparison of Muslims to Idolaters

The Wahhabis say: the defense of those who practice tawassul is the same apology the idolaters of the Arabs offered as the Qur'an says describing the way the idolaters defended their worship of idols: "We only worship them in order that they may bring us nearer" (39:3). Hence, the idolaters do not believe that the idols create anything. Rather, they believe that the Creator is God, the Exalted, by evidence of the following verse: "If thou ask them, Who created them, they will certainly say, God" (43:87) and: "If indeed thou ask them who is that created the heavens and the earth, they would be sure to say, God" (39:38). God has only judged against them for their disbelief because they say "We only worship them in order that they may bring us nearer." The Wahhabis say: Thus, do people who implore God by prophets and the pious use the phrase of the idolaters: "In order to bring us nearer" in the same sense.

Refutation of That False Comparison

The answer contains several points:

(1) The idolaters of the Arabs make idols gods; while the Muslims only believe in one God. In their view, prophets are prophets: awliya are awliya only. They do not adopt them as gods like the idolaters.

(2) The idolaters believe these gods deserve worship contrary to what Muslims believe. Muslims do not believe that anyone by whom they implore God deserve the least amount of worship. The only one entitled to worship in their view is God alone, May He be Exalted.

(3) The idolaters actually worship these gods as God relates: "We only *worship* them..." Muslims do not worship prophets and pious persons by the act of imploring God by means of them.

(4) The idolaters intend by their worship of their idols to draw near God just as He relates concerning them. As for the Muslims, they do not intend by imploring God by means of prophets and saints to draw close to God, which is only by worship. For that reason, God said in relating about the idolaters: "... in order that they bring us nearer." However, Muslims only intend blessings *(tabarruk)* and intercession *(shafa`a)* by them. Being blessed by a thing is obviously different from drawing near to God by it.

(5) Since the idolaters believe that God is a body in the sky, they mean by "to bring us near" a literal bringing near. What indicates this is its being stressed by their use of the word *zulfa* -- nearness to power -- inasmuch as emphasizing something by its own same meaning indicates for the most part that what is intended by it is the literal meaning and not the metaphorical. For when we say: "He slew him murderously" *(qatalahu qatlan)* a literal killing rushes to the understanding, not that of "a hard blow" in counterdistinction to what we mean when we just say: "He slew him"; for that might mean only a hard blow. The Muslims do not believe that God is a body in the sky remote enough from them to see a literal proximity to Him by imploring God through a prophet. The ruling of Shari`a contained in the verse does not apply to them, whereas since the Wahhabis believe that God is a body who sits on his throne, they do not discover a meaning of blessing which the Muslims intend by their imploring God by prophets and awliya, but only that of drawing near which belongs to bodies. For that reason, these verse are applicable to them not to Ahl al-Sunna.

Kinds of shirk We ought here to explain the various forms of idolatry or association of partners with God or shirk. First, we find the shirk of making-independent, such as affirming two independent gods like the shirk of the Zoroastrians. Secondly, there is the shirk of dividing into parts, that is, making-compound but of a number of gods like the shirk of the Christians. Thirdly, there is the shirk of drawing-near, that is, the worship of something other than God in order to draw near to God in a closer fashion. This is exemplified in the shirk of the Period of Ignorance prior to Islam.

The kind of shirk that Wahhabis made applicable to the Muslim making *istighatha* and *tawassul* and upon which Wahhabis built their doctrine of calling Muslims disbelievers belongs to the third category, the shirk of drawing-near which the *Jahiliyya* professed as its religion.

The state of affairs that delivered the Jahiliyya into its form of idolatry is a type of satanic seduction whereby its worship of God in its idolatrous manner stemmed from extreme human weakness and powerlessness; and a belief that not to draw near to Him by worshipping those nearest to Him, nobler in His sight, and more powerful, like the angels, would constitute bad manners. But when they observed the disappearance of the objects of their worship either constantly or some of the time they fashioned idols to represent them; so that when the objects of worship disappeared from them, they worshipped their images.

If this is firmly understood, then it is clear to the reader that the state of the idolaters of the Jahiliyya does not in any way apply to Muslims imploring God by the means of prophets and the pious. The Arabs of the Jahiliyya adopted idols as gods. "God" means "One who deserves worship." They believed the idols deserved worship. First of all, they believed that they could deliver harm and benefit. Thus, they worshipped them. This belief on their part plus their worship of them is what caused them to fall into idolatry. So when the proof was furnished them that these idols had no power to harm them or benefit them, they said: "We only worship in order that they bring us nearer." How, then, is it possible for the Wahhabis to assimilate the believers who declare that God is One to those idolaters of the Jahiliyya?

There is no doubt that Arab idolaters disbelieved simply because of their worship of statues and representations of prophets, angels, and awliya of which they formed images which they worshipped and to which they did sacrifice. This was due to their belief that prophets, angels, and awliya are gods *(aliha)* along with The God *(allah)* and could, on their own, do them benefit and harm. The God therefore furnished proof of the falsity of what they were saying and struck parables to refute their doctrine which He did in many verses. These verses state that the one God who alone is entitled to worship necessarily has power over removing harm and delivering benefit to him who worships Him; and that what they in fact worshipped were objects originating in time and antithetical to Lordship. Persons who seek help and who call upon God by means of prophets are free and innocent of this order of idolatrous worship and belief.

As for the claim that seeking aid *(istighatha)* is worship of someone other than God, it is high-handed and arbitrary. For the verses which the Wahhabis adduce as proof-texts -- all of them -- were revealed to apply to unbelievers who worship someone other than God. They intended by their worship of that other individual to come closer to Him. Furthermore, they believed that there is another god along with God and that He has a son and a wife -- exalted exceedingly high is He beyond what they say. This is a point of unanimous agreement which no one disputes. There is nothing in the verses revealed concerning the unbelievers that would count as evidence that merely seeking the help of a prophet or saint when accompanied by faith in God is worship of someone other than God Himself.

Refutation of their claim that tawassul is worship of other than God

The Wahhabis say that such seeking of help is a form of invocation. They cite the hadith: "*inna al-du`a huwa al-`ibada*": "Invocation -- it is worship."[45] Hence, they claim, he who asks help from a prophet or a saint *(wali)* is simply worshipping him by that

---

[45]Ahmad 4:267, 271, 276; Tirmidhi, Tafsir of surat 2:16 (#2969) and 40 (#3247, #3372) (hasan sahih); Abu Dawud Witr # 1479 (sahih); Ibn Hibban; Bukhari in *al-Adab al-mufrad* (sahih); Ibn Majah, Du`a Ch. 1 (#3828), and Bayhaqi in *Shu`ab al-iman* 2:37 (#1105bis);

request for help; yet only worship of God alone is beneficial and worship of other than Him is *shirk*. Hence, they conclude, the one who seeks aid of someone other than Him is an idolater.

The answer for this is that the verbal pronoun *huwa* ("it is") in the hadith conveys restriction of the grammatical predicate "worship" to its subject "invocation" and it thus renders definite the predicate, just as the author of *al-Miftah*[46] says and with whom the majority of the scholars agree concerning this hadith. Thus, for example, when we say: "God -- He is the Provider" *(Allah huwa al-Razzaq)* (51:58), it means there is no provider other than He. Accordingly, when the Prophet said: "Invocation: it is worship" he signified that worship is restricted to invocation. What is meant by the hadith is:

"Worship is nothing other than invocation."

And the Qur'an supports this meaning when it says: "Say: My Lord would not concern Himself with you but for your call *(du`a)* on Him" (25:77). That is, He would not have shown favor to you were it not for your worship. For the honor of mankind lies in its worship and its respect in its knowledge and obedience. Otherwise, man would not be superior to the beasts. The Hajj, the Zakat, the Fast and the testimony of faith are all invocation and likewise reading of the Qur'an, *dhikr* or remembrance, and obedience. Hence, worship is confined to invocation. Once this is firmly established, it becomes clear that there no is proof in the hadith for what Wahhabis claim, because if asking for help is a kind of invocation, as the Wahhabis claim, it does not necessarily follow that asking for help is worship, since invocation is not always worship as is plain to see.[47]

If, on the contrary, we restrict the subject "invocation" to the predicate "worship" in the hadith according to the interpretation

---

without "inna": Muslim, Tabarani, al-Hakim, al-Nisa'i, and Ibn Abi Shayba.

[46]Suyuti: *Miftah al jannah fi al-i`tisam bi al-sunnah.*

[47]E.g. in the sense of calling someone.

of the author of *al-Kashshaf*[48] whereby the definition of the predicate in a nominal clause might be either restricted to the subject or restricted to the predicate, then the logical deduction of the Wahhabis whereby all du`a is worship is still not supported by it. Otherwise, the definite article *al* in *al-du`a* (invocation or literally a call on someone) makes invocation generic and betokens universal inclusion into the genus. Yet this is not the case since not every invocation is an act of worship *(`ibada)*.

On the contrary, the matter stands as we find it in the verse of Qur'an: "Nor call on other than God such as can neither profit thee nor hurt thee" (10:106) and similarly in the verse: "Call your witnesses or helpers!" (2:23). Calling on God in the sense of requesting is found where the Qur'an says: "Call on Me and I will answer you" (40:60) and in the sense of a declarative statement: "This will be their prayer *(da`wahum)* therein: Glory to Thee, O God!" (10:10). As for "calling on someone" in the sense of summoning them *(nida')*, we find: "It will be on the day when he will call you *(yad`ukum)*" (17:52) and in the sense of naming someone we find: "Deem not the calling *(du`a)* of the Messenger of God among yourselves like the calling of one of you to another" (24:63).

As the author of *al-Itqan*[49] makes plain: If the definite article belongs to the genus and signifies universal inclusion therein, then the man who says: "Zayd! Give me a dirham" perpetrates an act of disbelief. Yet the Wahhabis, of course, will not claim this. Hence, it is plain that the definite article signifies specification. So what is meant by invocation in the hadith is *invocation to God* and not calling on someone in the general sense. The meaning would be:

"Calling to God is one of the greatest acts of worship."

---

[48]al-Zamakhshari's Qur'anic commentary entitled *al-Kashshaf `an haqaiq al-tanzil wa-`uyun al-aqawil fi wujuh al-ta'wil.*

[49]Suyuti: *al-Itqan fi `ulum al-Qur'an.*

It is in the manner of the Prophet's saying: "*al-hajju `arafatun*" or:

"The Pilgrimage is `Arafah"[50]

which is taken to mean that this represents the Hajj's greatest essential element. For the one making the request comes toward God and turns aside from what is other than He. Furthermore, the request is commanded by God and the action fulfilling that command is worship. The Prophet names it "worship" to show the subjugation of the subject making the request, the indigence of his condition, and the humility and lowliness of his worship.

Among the proofs that what is meant by "invocation" in the hadith is the "calling on God" and not the general sense of "calling" is the fact which many grammarians confirm and Ibn Rushd clearly makes plain as does al-Qarafi also in his Commentary on *al-Tanqih*:[51] namely, that asking *(al-su'al)* is one of the categories of wanting *(al-talab)* put forth by one lower to one higher in station. If it is addressed to God, it is named "request" *(su'al)* and "invocation" *(du`a)*. The latter is not applied to someone other than God. And if it is not permissible *(la yajuz)* to name the request of other than God by the unqualified name of *du`a*, then such a request *a fortiori* is not named a *du`a* in the sense of worship.

10: Tawassul (Using means): Evidence for its Permissibility

Before plunging into this chapter let us clarify one thing pertaining to what one means by seeking help with the prophets and pious persons and imploring God by means of them. First, they are means and causes to obtain what is intended. Second, God is the true agent of the favor or miracle which comes at their hand, not they themselves, just as true doctrine asserts in the case of other actions: for the knife does not

---

[50]Tirmidhi, Tafsir 2:22; Abu Dawud, Manasik 68; Ibn Majah, Manasik 57; Darimi, Manasik 54.

[51]This is *Sharh tanqih al-fusul fi al-usul* by Ahmad ibn Idris al-Qarafi al-Maliki (d. 1285 CE).

cut by itself but the cutter is God the Exalted, although the agent is the knife in the domain of the customary connection of events. Be that as it may, it is God who creates the cutting.

Al-Subki, al-Qastallani in *al-Mawahib al-laduniyya*, al-Samhudi in *Tarikh al-Madina*, and al-Haythami in *al-Jawhar al-munazzam* said that seeking help with the Prophet and other prophets and pious persons, is only a means of imploring God for the sake of their dignity and honor *(bi jahihim)*. The one doing the asking seeks from the One asked that He assign him aid *(ghawth)* on behalf of the one higher than him. For the one being asked in reality is God. The Prophet is but the intermediary means *(wasita)* between the one asking for help and the One asked in reality. Hence, the help is strictly from Him in its creation *(khalqan)* and being *(ijadan)*, while the help from the Prophet is strictly in respect to secondary causation *(tasabbuban)* and acquisition from God *(kasban)*.

The most prominent among the scholars of Islam have acknowledged the permissibility of *istighatha* and *tawassul* with the Prophet, peace be upon him.[52] Its permissibility is not

---

[52]Imam Ahmad, for example. `Ala' al-Din al-Mardawi said in his book *al-insaf fi ma`rifat al-rajih min al-khilaf `ala madhhab al-Imam al-mubajjal Ahmad ibn Hanbal* (3:456): "The correct position of the [Hanbali] madhhab is that it is permissible in one's supplication (du`a) to use as means a pious person, and it is said that it is desirable (mustahabb). Imam Ahmad said to al-Marwadhi: *yatawassalu bi al-nabi fi du`a'ih* -- "Let him use the Prophet as a means in his supplication to God.""

Al-hafiz Taqi al-Din al-Subki said: "Verily God knows that every goodness in my life which He has bestowed upon me is on account of the Prophet (s), that my recourse is to him, and that my reliance is upon him in seeking a means to God in every matter of mine. Verily he is my means to God in this world and the next." In *Fatawa al-Subki*, beginning of the article entitled "The Descent of Tranquility and Peace on the Nightlights of Madina" (tanazzul al-sakina `ala qanadil al-madina) 1:274.

contravened by the report of Abu Bakr, may God be pleased with him, whereby when he said "Rise! [plural], We will seek help with the Messenger of God from this hypocrite," the Prophet said:

> "*Innahu la yustaghathu bi innama yustaghathu billah*"
>
> "Help is not sought with me, it is sought only with God."

Since Ibn Luhay`a is part of its chain of transmission, the discussion of it is well-known.[53]

Were we to suppose that the hadith is sound, it would be of the like of the Qur'anic verse, "You did not throw when you threw, but God threw" (8:17)[54] and the Prophet said, "I did not bear you but God bore you."[55] Thus the meaning of the hadith "Help is not sought with me" is:

> "(Even if I am the one ostensibly being asked
> for help,) I am not the one being asked for help,
> in reality God Himself is being asked."

Imam Shawkani said in his commentary on al-Jazari's (d. 833) *'Iddat al-hisn al-hasin* entitled *Tuhfat al-dhakirin bi `iddat al-hisn al-hasin*: "He [al-Jazari] said: Let him make tawassul to God with His Prophets and the *salihin* or saints (in his du`a). I say: And exemplifying tawassul with the Prophets is the hadith extracted by Tirmidhi *et al.* (of the blind man saying: O Allah, I ask You and turn to You by means of Muhammad the Prophet of Mercy)... as for tawassul with the saints, among its examples is the hadith, established as sound, of the Companions' tawassul asking God for rain by means of al-`Abbas the Prophet's uncle, and `Umar said: "O Allah, we use as means to You the uncle of our Prophet etc." (Beirut ed. 1970) p. 37.

[53]Suyuti, *Jami` al-ahadith* 496 #2694. Haythami in *Majma` al-zawa'id*: "Tabarani related it and its men are those of sound hadith except Ibn Luhay`a who is fair (hasan).

[54]And: "Those who swear allegiance unto thee swear allegiance only unto God" (48:10).

[55]Bukhari and Muslim.

In sum, the term *istighatha* or "asking for help" applies to whomever the help comes from including in respect to causation and acquisition;[56] this is what the Arabic means and the Shari`a permits. The hadith "Help is not sought with me" must be interpreted in the light of this. This meaning is supported by the hadith in *Sahih al-Bukhari*[57] touching on intercession on the Day of Resurrection. Such was the help people sought from Adam, then Ibrahim, then Musa, then `Isa, then Muhammad, on him and them be God's blessings and peace.

Now we have come to the point of setting forth the permissibility of tawassul and adducing evidence for it. We find in the Qur'an:

> "O ye who believe! Be wary of God and seek *al-wasila* -- the means to approach Him" (5:35).

Ibn `Abbas said that *al-wasila* signifies whatever means one employs to draw close to God. The Wahhabis claim that "means" refers exclusively to actions and this is pure arbitrariness. The manifest and apparent sense *(zahir)* of the text refers to persons *(dhawat)* not actions. For God says: *ittaqu Allah* (Fear God) which conveys the sense of wariness in doing whatever God has ordered and relinquishing whatever He has forbidden. If we interpret "seek the means" in terms of actions, then the order of "seeking the means" would consist in an emphasis *(ta'kid)* of the command: "Be wary of God." This is different than if "seeking the means" is interpreted to refer to persons. For then the command of *taqwa* is to actually lay a basis *(ta'sis)* for one's action and this is better than emphasis.[58]

---

[56] I.e. secondary causes.

[57] Kitab al-Tawhid.

[58] To be wary of God is itself a means to Him, therefore the order that follows it ("Seek a means to Him"), if it refers to actions, is a reiteration of the action already named ("Fear God") for emphasis. This Zahawi calls *ta'kid*. If it refers to persons, however, it is a definition of a distinct action rather than a reiteration of the action already named. This

Again, God says:

> "Those unto whom they cry seek for themselves the means of approach to their Lord, which of them shall be the nearest" (17:57).

Ibn `Abbas said they are Jesus and his mother, Azrael and the angels. And the commentary on this verse is that the unbelievers worship prophets and angels because they regard them as their lords. Thus God says to them, "Those whom you worship are imploring God by who is nearer. How, then, do you make them lords when they are servants in need of their Lord and imploring Him by One who is higher in rank than they are?"

God also said:

> "If they had only, when they were unjust to themselves, come unto thee and asked God's forgiveness, and then the Messenger had asked forgiveness for them, they would have found God indeed Oft-returning, Most Merciful" (4:64).

God has linked their seeking of forgiveness from Him with seeking forgiveness from the Prophet. So in this verse from the Qur'an we have clear evidence of imploring God by means of the Prophet and acceptance of the one that implores Him in this fashion. We understand this also from the statement: "They would have found God Oft-returning, Most Merciful."

Asking forgiveness for his community, you should know, is not tied to his being alive and the hadiths cited shortly indicate this. One cannot say that the verses cited among a definite group of people have no general applicability; for even if they are cited among a definite group while the Prophet was alive, they maintain a

---

Zahawi calls *ta'sis*. In the latter case the strength of the two orders is greater.

general relevance by the generality of the cause occasioning their utterance. So the verses take in whomever satisfies such a description whether he be alive or dead.[59]

Another evidence is the Qur'anic verse: "Now the man of his own people appealed to him [Musa] against his foe" (28:15). Here God attributes a request for help to a creature who is asking someone other than Himself. This is sufficient evidence for the permissibility for asking someone other than God for help.

If someone objects and says that the help being sought in these texts is from someone alive and who has power over his actions, the reply is that attributing the power to him if it is held to issue from him in a fashion independent of Divine assistance is the

---

[59] Al-`Utbi said: As I was sitting by the grave of the Prophet (s), a Beduin Arab came and said: "Peace be upon you, O Messenger of God! I have heard God saying: "If they had only, when they were unjust to themselves, come unto thee and asked Allah's forgiveness, and the Messenger had asked forgiveness for them, they would have found Allah indeed Oft-returning, Most Merciful" (4:64), so I have come to you asking forgiveness (of God) for my sin, seeking your intercession with my Lord." Then he began to recite poetry:

O best of those whose bones are buried in the deep earth,
And from whose fragrance the depth and height have become sweet,
May I be the ransom for a grave which thou inhabit,
And in which are found purity and bounty and munificence!

Then he left, and I dozed and saw the Prophet (s) in my sleep. He said to me: "O `Utbi, run after the Beduin and give him glad tidings that God has forgiven him."

Related in: Nawawi, *Adhkar*, Mecca ed. p. 253-254, and *al-Idah fi manasik al-hajj*, chapter on visiting the Prophet; Ibn Hajar al-Haythami, *al-Jawhar al-munazzam* [commentary on Nawawi's *Idah*]; al-Qurtubi, commentary on 4:64 in *Ahkam al-Qur'an* 5:265; Samhudi, *Khulasat al-Wafa* p. 121 (from Nawawi); Dahlan, *Khulasat al-Kalam* 2:247; Ibn Kathir, *Tafsir* 4:64 and *al-Bidayat wa al-nihayat* 1:180; Abu Muhammad ibn Qudama, *al-Mughni* 3:556; Abu al-Faraj ibn Qudama, *al-Sharh al-kabir* 3:495; al-Bahooti al-Hanbali, *Kashshaf al-qina`* 5:30; Taqi al-Din al-Subki, *Shifa' al-siqam* p. 52; and Ibn al-Jawzi, *Muthir al-gharam al-sakin ila ashraf al-amakin*.

same as *kufr*, that is disbelief. And if it is only God's power to be a cause and means, then there is no difference between living and dead. Thus the recipient, alive or dead, possesses the miracle as a token of respect and honor. If the seeking of aid is not related to God literally and to someone else figuratively, the seeking of help is forbidden in either case. From this you know the secret of the Prophet's formal rejection of seeking help from himself when Abu Bakr al-Siddiq said: "Rise! We will ask the Messenger of God for help from this hypocrite" and the Messenger of God said to him: "Help is not sought from me. Help is sought from God" despite the fact that the Prophet was then alive and had power over his actions. He only intended to deny the seeking of help from him literally and in reality. For he wanted to teach his Community that help only can be sought, in reality, from God.

We find another evidence for *tawassul* in the Qur'anic verse:

> "They do not possess intercession save those
> who have made a covenant with their Lord" (19:87).

Some of the commentators on Qur'an say that the "covenant" *(al-`ahd)* is the phrase: "There is no god but God and Muhammad is the Messenger of God." The meaning of the verse would be: "Intercessors will not intercede except for those who say: There is no god but God," that is, the believers, like what we find where the Qur'an says: "They only intercede for one who is accepted" (21:28). However, the resulting meaning: they do not possess intercession for anyone except those who made a covenant etc. is far-fetched and somewhat constrained.

The best commentary of God's statement "They do not possess" is "They do not obtain." Then, the expression of the exception "save those who..." is admissible without implying something in addition, and the meaning is asserted: "He does not possess intercession except the one who says: There is no god but God." That is, only the believers intercede. This is like the verse "And those unto whom they call instead of Him possess no power of intercession except him who bears witness to the Truth" (43:86). The bearing witness to the Truth is the phrase: "There is no god but God."

Since what is meant by imploring God with the prophets, the saints, and the pious and by asking them for help is a request for their intercession, and since God has related that they possess intercession, then who can prevent anyone from seeking by permission of God what they possess by permission of God? Thus, it is permissible to ask from them that they give you what God has given to them. The only thing forbidden is asking intercession from idols which do not possess anything at all.

Another evidence is narrated by Ibn Majah with a sound chain of transmission on the authority of Abu Sa`id al-Khudri, may God be pleased with him. He relates that the Messenger of God said: "The one who leaves his house for prayer and then says: "O God, I ask thee by the right of those who ask you and I beseech thee by the right of those who walk this path unto thee, as my going forth bespeak not of levity, pride nor vainglory, nor is done for the sake of repute. I have gone forth solely in the warding off your anger and for the seeking of your pleasure. I ask you, therefore, to grant me refuge from hell fire and to forgive me my sins. For no one forgive sins but yourself." God will look kindly upon him and seventy thousand angels will seek his forgiveness."[60]

In this manner did the Prophet make tawassul when he said "I ask thee by the right of those who ask you," that is, by every believing servant. Moreover, he commanded his Companions to use this prayer when they made du`a and to make tawassul just as he

---

[60]Related in *Musnad* Ahmad (3:21), Ibn Majah (Masajid), al-Mundhiri in *al-Targhib* (1:179), Ibn Khuzayma in his *Sahih*, Ibn al-Sani, and Abu Nu`aym. Ghazali mentions it in the *Ihya* and `Iraqi said: it is hasan. Nawawi mentions Ibn al-Sani's two chains in the *Adhkar* and says they are weak. However, Ibn Hajar al-`Asqalani says it is hasan in *al-Amali al-masriyya* (#54) and the *Takhrij* of Nawawi's book, explaining that the latter neglected Abu Sa`id al-Khudri's narration and omitted to mention Ibn Majah's.

made tawassul. The Pious Ancestors (al-Salaf) of our faith among the Companions' Successors and their Successors continued to use this prayer upon their going out to prayer and no one disavowed them for it.

Among further evidences for the permissibility of tawassul is the occasion when the Prophet said on the authority of Anas ibn Malik: "O God, grant forgiveness to my mother, Fatima Bint Asad, and make vast for her the place of her going in[61] by right of thy Prophet and that of those prophets who came before me" and so on until the end of the hadith. Al-Tabarani relates it in *al-Kabir*. Ibn Hibban and al-Hakim declare it sound. The "Fatima" referred to here is the mother of Sayyidina `Ali who raised the Prophet. Ibn Abi Shayba on the authority of Jabir relates a similar narrative. Similar also is what Ibn `Abd Al-Barr on the authority of Ibn `Abbas and Abu Nu`aym in his *Hilya* on the authority of Anas Ibn Malik relate, as al-Hafiz al-Suyuti mentioned in the *Jami` al-Kabir*.[62]

Also found as evidence: al-Tirmidhi, al-Nasa'i, al-Bayhaqi, and al-Tabarani relate with a sound chain that a blind man came to the Prophet and said: "Pray to God that He relieve me." The Prophet said: "If you wish I will pray, and if you wish you may be patient, and that is better." Then he prayed for him and commanded him to make ablution and do his ablution well and utter this prayer: "O God, I ask you and I address You by Your Prophet Muhammad, the Prophet of Mercy. O Muhammad, I address by you my Lord in my need. O God, accept his intercession on my behalf." Then he returned and gained his sight. Al-Bukhari produces this hadith in his *Ta'rikh* (Biographical History), Ibn Majah, and al-Hakim in *al-Mustadrak* with a sound chain of transmission. Suyuti in *al-Jami' al-Kabir* and *al-Saghir* mentioned it also. It is therefore established

---

[61] I.e. her grave.

[62] Haythami says in *Majma` al-zawa'id*: "Tabarani's chain contains Rawh ibn Salah who has some weakness but Ibn Hibban and al-Hakim declared him trustworthy. The rest of its sub-narrators are the men of sound hadith."

that the Prophet commanded the blind man to invoke him and implore God by means of him to accomplish his need.

The Wahhabis may claim that this is only in the life of the Prophet and that it does not provide evidence for the permissibility of imploring God by means of him after death. We answer that this prayer has been used by the Companions and the Successors also after the repose of the Prophet to accomplish their needs. The evidence for this is what al-Tabarani and al-Bayhaqi have related, namely, that a man visited `Uthman ibn `Affan, may God be pleased with him, during the time when he was Caliph, concerning a certain need he had but the noble Commander of the Faithful did not look immediately into it. The man complained to `Uthman Ibn Hunayf who said to him: "Go and make ablution, then go to the mosque and pray in the following manner: "O God, I ask you and address you by your Prophet Muhammad, the Prophet of Mercy. O Muhammad, I address my Lord by you to accomplish my need." Then mention your need." So the man went away and did precisely as he was told and came back to the door of `Uthman ibn `Affan. Then the doorkeeper came to him, took his hand, brought him into the presence of `Uthman and made him to sit down with him. `Uthman said: "Tell me what you need" and he mentioned his need and it was fulfilled. Then the Caliph said to him: "Whatever need you have, mention it to me." When the man went out of his presence he met Ibn Hunayf and said: "May God reward you with good for he would have not looked into my need until you spoke to him for me." But Ibn Hunayf said: "By God I did not speak to him, but I witnessed God's Messenger when the blind man came to him and complained about losing his sight."[63]

Such an act constitutes tawassul and he called upon him after the death of the Prophet on the grounds that the Prophet is living in his grave and his rank is above the rank of the Martyrs

---

[63]Sound (sahih) hadith related by Bayhaqi, Abu Nu`aym in the *Ma`rifa*, Mundhiri (*Targhib* 1:473-474), Haythami, and Tabarani in the *Kabir* (9:17-18) and the *Saghir* (1:184/201-202) on the authority of `Uthman ibn Hunayf's nephew Abu Imama ibn Sahl ibn Hunayf.

whom God has expressly said that they are living, being provided for, with their Lord.

Another evidence for tawassul is what al-Bayhaqi and Ibn Abi Shayba relate with a sound chain of transmission that a drought afflicted the people during the caliphate of `Umar, may God be pleased with him, and Bilal Ibn al-Harth came to the grave of the Prophet and said: "O Messenger of God, ask for rain for your community, for they are being destroyed." Then the Messenger of God came to him in a dream and said to him that they would have water. This evidence of ours is not in the vision of the Prophet. Even if his vision is true, the legal rulings of the Shari`a are not established by dreams, where there is room to cast doubt on the words or perspicuity of the dreamer. The evidence we are citing lies in the action of one of the Companions while that Companion was awake. That is Bilal Ibn al-Harth who came to the grave of the Prophet and called on him and made a request of him to provide his community with rain.[64]

Again, we find evidence in the *Sahih* of Bukhari from a narration of Anas Ibn Malik from `Umar Ibn al-Khattab in the time when he was Caliph asking for rain by means of al-`Abbas, the uncle of the Prophet, when there was a drought in the Year of "Ramada" (the Year of Destruction in 17 A.H.), then they received

---

[64]Ibn Kathir cites it from Bayhaqi in *al-bidaya wa al-nihaya* (7:92) and says: *isnaduhu sahih*; Ibn Abi Shayba cites it in his "Musannaf" with a sound (sahih) chain as confirmed by Ibn Hajar who says: *rawa Ibn Abi Shayba bi isnadin sahih* and cites the hadith in *Fath al-bari* Istisqa' ch. 3 (Beirut: Dar al-kutub al-`ilmiyya, 1410/1989 2:629-630). Ibn Hajar says that the man who visited and saw the Prophet (s) in his dream is identified as the Companion Bilal ibn al-Harth. He counts this hadith as one of the reason for Bukhari's naming of the chapter "The people's request to their leader for rain if they suffer drought."

In his edition of Ibn Hajar, the Wahhabi scholar Ibn Baz rejects the hadith as a valid source for seeking rain through the Prophet (s) -- although it is established that the hadith is sound -- and condemns the act of the Companion who came to the grave, calling it "*munkar*" and "*wasilat ila al-shirk.*" *Fath al-Bari* 2:630n.

rain. And in *al-Mawahib al-laduniyya* of the savant al-Qastallani we find that when `Umar asked `Abbas for rain, he said: "O people, the Messenger of God used to see in al-`Abbas what as son sees in a father," whereupon they followed the Prophet's model in his behavior with al-`Abbas and took the latter as a means to God.

There is no difference in the tawassul or imploring by naming prophets and other pious persons and them being alive or dead because in neither state do they differ in anything whatsoever. In either state, producing an effect on states of affairs is not up to them. Creation, bringing into existence, producing an effect on states of affairs: all of this belongs to God alone, who has no partner in this or anything else. As for the one who believes that producing effects belongs only to the living, it is up to them to differentiate between imploring God for the sake of the living or imploring God for the sake of the dead. For our part we say that God is the Creator of all things regardless, and "God has created you and all you do" (37:96). The Wahhabis who make a great show of their defense of monotheism and permit using only living persons as a means have made themselves fall into the sin of associating a partner with God *(shirk)* insofar as they believe, in their ignorance, that living beings have an effect upon things when in reality no one produces an effect except God.

Using as means *(tawassul)*, or using as intermediary *(tashaffu`)*, or asking for help *(istighatha)* a single person: the upshot of all this is the same, the aim of it being only to get blessings *(tabarruk)* by mentioning the names of beloved servants of God for whose sake God may grant mercy to creation, be they living or dead. The actual author of existence is God alone, they are only customary causes *(asbab `adiyya)*, they produce no effect on their own.

Their Condemnation of *Nida'* (Calling Out)

As for the invocations of common Muslim people in Arabic like: "O `Abd al-Qadir Gilani look at me *(Ya `Abd al-Qadir adrikni)*!" and "O Ahmad al-Badawi give us support *(Ya Badawi madad)*!" they belong to the figurative language of the mind just as the application of someone who says to his food: "Satisfy me!" or to his water: "Quench my thirst!" or to his medicine: "Heal me!" The food does not satisfy, nor does the water quench the thirst, nor the medicine heal. But the One who is the real Satisfier of our hunger, the Quencher of our thirst and the Healer of our ills is God alone. The food, the water, the medicine are only the proximate or secondary causes which custom has established on the surface of things by our mind's regular association of them with certain concomitant events.

The majority of the Muslim community agree on the permissibility of imploring God for the sake of the Prophet, the Companions, and the pious. From many of the Companions, the ulama of the Pious Ancestors, and those in succeeding generations, the meeting together of a majority on what is forbidden and idolatrous is not allowable because of the Prophet's sound hadith which some consider *mutawatir*:[65] "My community will not come together on an error"[66] and because God said: "You are the best community of mankind which has been produced" (3:110). Then how could all of them or the majority of them come together on what is erroneous?

One of the evidences permitting the seeking of help is what Bukhari has related in a sound hadith from Ibn `Abbas that the Prophet mentioned in the story of Hajar, the mother of Isma`il: when thirst overtook her and her son, she began to run in search for water, then she heard a voice yet saw no one and she said: "If there be help *(ghawth)* with you, then help us *(aghith)*."[67] If seeking aid of other than God was *shirk* then why did she seek aid? Why did the Prophet mention it to his Companions and not reject it? And why did the Companions after him transmit it and the narrators of hadith mention it?

---

[65]I.e. of definite authenticity and commanding belief.
[66]Already referenced in the section on *ijma`*.
[67]*Sahih al-Bukhari*, Kitab al-anbiya'.

Bukhari also relates in the Hadith of Intercession[68] that people, while they are in the horrors in the Day of Resurrection, ask help of Adam, then of Noah, then of Abraham, then of Moses, then of Jesus, and all of them will give an excuse, and Jesus will say: "Go to Muhammad." Then they will go to Muhammad and then he will say: "I will do it." If seeking aid of a creature was forbidden then the Prophet would have not mentioned to the Companions. The ones who object to this give the answer that this is the Day of Resurrection when the Prophet has power. One responds with the refutation that in their worldly life they have no power except as a secondary cause: likewise after death, the living in their graves and beyond are allowed to be secondary causes only.

Al-Tabarani has related from `Utba Ibn Ghazwan from the Prophet that he said: "If one of you loses his way with respect to anything whatsoever or wishes help when he is in a land in which he has no friend let him say: O servants of God help me *(ya `ibad Allah a`inuni)*! for God has servants whom he does not see."[69]

---

[68]Kitab al-tawhid.

[69]Hadith hasan (fair) related by Tabarani in *al-Kabir*, Abu Ya`la, Ibn al-Sani, and Haythami in *Majma` al-zawa'id* 10:132. Bayhaqi relates something close to it on the authority of Ibn `Abbas in *Kitab al-adaab*" (p. 436): "God has angels on earth who keep a record even of the leaves that falls on the ground. Therefore, if one of you has a lameness in his leg or finds himself in need in a deserted place of the earth, let him say: *a`inu `ibad Allah rahimakum Allah*, "Help, O servants of Allah, may Allah have mercy on you!" Verily he shall be helped, if God wills." Ibn Hajar said its chain is fair *(isnaduhu hasan)* in *al-Amali*. Bayhaqi relates it with two more chains from Ibn `Abbas in *Shu`ab al-iman* (1:183 #167; 6:128 #7697) and another from Ibn Mas`ud in *Hayat al-anbiya' ba`da wafatihim* (p. 44) also related in *al-Kabir* by Tabarani who has *ya `ibad Allah a`inu* repeated three times, Ibn al-Sani, Abu Ya`la, and Nawawi in *al-Adhkar*. Ibn Abi Shayba relates in his *Musannaf* (7:103) through Aban ibn Salih that the Prophet (s) said: "If one of you loses his animal or his camel in a deserted land where there is no-one in sight, let him say: "O servants of Allah, help me! *(a`inu `ibad Allah)*, for verily he will be helped." The latter is the same as Bayhaqi's narration #167 from Ibn `Abbas.

It is not said that all that is meant by the "servants of God" in the hadith cited above are only angels, or Muslims among the jinn, or men of the realm of the invisible: for all of these are living.[70] Hence, the hadith would not give evidence for asking aid from the dead, but this is not the case. We mention this because there is nothing explicit in the hadith whereby what is meant by "servants of God" are the categories we mentioned above and nothing else. Yet even if we were to concede this, the hadith would still be a proof against the Wahhabis from another standpoint, and that is the calling on someone invisible. The Wahhabis no more allow it than the calling on the dead.[71]

Furthermore, their contestation for some of the narrators of this hadith is pointless. It was narrated through a variety of paths of transmission, one of which supports the other. Thus, al-Hakim related it in his book of sound hadith as well as Abu `Uwana and al-Bazzar with a sound chain of transmission from the Prophet in this form: "If the mount of one of you runs loose in a desert land, let him call: O servants of God, restrain my beast! *(ya `ibad Allah ahbisu)*." Shaykh al-Islam Ibn Taymiyya has mentioned this hadith in his book *al-Kalim al-Tayyib*, also Ibn Qayyim in his own *al-Kalim al-Tayyib*, Nawawi in his *Adhkar*, al-Jazari in *Al-Hisn al-Hasin*, and other transmitters of hadith whose number is too large to count. The latter wording is from the narrative of Ibn Mas`ud whose chain of transmission is continuous back to the Prophet. The narration of Ibn Mas`ud whose chain is interrupted is: "Let him call: O servants of God, help me *(a`inuni ya `ibad Allah)*."[72]

---

[70]I.e. there is no controversy about asking their help.

[71]Shawkani allows the calling on someone invisible: "In the hadith (of *a`inu*) there is evidence that it is permissible to ask help from those one does not see among the servants of God, whether angels or good jinn, and there is nothing wrong in doing it, just as it is permissible for someone to seek the help of human beings if his mount becomes unmanageable or runs loose." *Tuhfat al-dhakirin* p. 155-156.

[72]Ibn Mas`ud's narration of *ahbisu* is the weaker of the chains and `Utba's narration of *a`inu* the stronger. Ibn Hajar said of the former, as reported by Ibn `Allan in his *Futuhat* (5:145): "A rare (gharib) hadith related by Ibn al-Sani (#508) and Tabarani (cf. Munawi in *Fayd al-*

There is also transmitted on the authority of `Abd Allah Ibn al-Imam Ahmad Ibn Hanbal that he said: "I heard my father say: "I had made Hajj five times and once I got lost on the way. I was walking and I began to say: O servants of God, show us the way! I continued to say this until I got on the right way."[73]

One of the Wahhabis' pretexts in declaring disbeliever anyone who asks for help or calls on an absent prophet or saint who has died is that the call of people who beseech help from an absent prophet or saint might be in numerous places at one and the same time, and the number of the callers exceedingly large, mounting to hundreds of thousands. Yet and still, they claim, the ones asking for help believe that the one who is called upon is present at that very moment -- not to mention their view that it is disbelief and *shirk* because of attributing to the person called upon for help the characteristics of God, since they are impossible for the ordinary mind to conceive when attributed to a human being. For it is obvious that one body cannot be existent in numerous places at one time.

The answer is that Muslims do not believe that the person called upon is present in person at the time he is called in a number

---

Qadir 1:307) and its chain is interrupted." Both Ibn Hajar and al-Haythami (*Majma`* 10:132) said: "Its chain contains Ma`ruf ibn Hassan who is weak." (Shawkani mentions that Abu Ya`la cites it also.) However, as the third previous note shows, the hadith *a`inu* is established as authentic.

Nawawi relates in *Al-adhkar* after mentioning the hadith *ahbisu*: "One of our very knowledgeable teachers related to me that one day his animal ran loose -- I think it was a mule -- and he knew that hadith, so he said it, and Allah restrained it for them on the spot. I myself was with a group one time when one of their animals broke free and they were unable to restrain it, so I said it: it stopped on the spot with no reason other than those words." Shawkani cites Nawawi's two accounts in his *Tuhfat al-dhakirin*.

[73]Reported by Ibn Muflih al-Hanbali in his book *al-Adaab al-shar`iyya*.

of places. That counts as disbelief. Besides, omnipresence of this order is impossible. What the callers believe is that the *baraka*, that is, the blessing or grace of the one called, is present in those places in a subtle fashion by God's act of creation and motivated by His mercy for the person asking for help out of respect for the one whom he calls on. That is not impossible, for the mercy of God is wide and without limit.

Then, when the Wahhabis attribute to Muslims this belief (omnipresence in person) of which they are completely innocent, they apply to it the criterion of invalidity which the jurists apply in the conditions of marriage if, as they note, a man marries a woman "by witness of God *and* his Messenger": the marriage contract is invalid. The Wahhabis then claim: if the Prophet knows of the call of someone who is asking for help when he calls out to him from afar, then he would be the Knower of the invisible and the contract of marriage which the jurists say is invalid would be sound.

The answer is that Muslims just as they do not believe the Prophet or a saint asked for help is present when he is called; likewise they do not attribute knowledge of the invisible to anyone except God, the Exalted. As for the absence of the validity of a marriage contract by witness of God *and* His Messenger, it is because Islamic Law makes the eye-witness testimony a condition of marriage and acts like it to preserve the marriage rights; since disputes may arise between the partners to the marriage which may eventually come before judges. Then it will be impossible for one or the other of the disputing parties to establish his claim by the witness of God and His Messenger. For suppose that God -- who transcends what the obscurantists say -- is indeed a body who comes down to the lower heaven as the Wahhabis claim: then we would say it would be a common phenomenon for him to descend to the courtroom so that His testimony before it might be produced to decisively settle the dispute of the two contending parties!

You know that the Wahhabis declare one who calls on other than God a disbeliever; for example, one who says "O Messenger of God" *(ya rasulallah)* and so forth. Yet if we go to look we see that this purported disbelief of one who says "O Messenger of God!" for example, implies two suppositions: either he believes that the individual whom he calls is himself present at the time of his call, hears his call, accomplishes his need because of it and saves him from the difficulty for which he called him in the first place; or he believes that the one whom he calls hears by God's hearing, purely through God's own power, and that God and no one else accomplished his need in virtue of the baraka of the one on whom he calls; and, moreover, that it is God who delivers him from the difficulty which he is in, for the honor of that Prophet.

Either supposition shows some fault of thinking on the part of the Wahhabi who claims that the caller is a disbeliever. As for the first, anyone who believes that someone else other than God accomplishes his need and saves him from difficulty is a disbeliever *whether he calls out or never calls out anyone* and it is incorrect to make his disbelief depend on the circumstance of calling out. You know that no Muslim believes this doctrine. As for the second supposition, one whose heart is the seat of faith[74] and who believes that the one who accomplishes needs and saves from perils is God alone, not someone else: it is not allowed that such a person be called an unbeliever solely on the basis of calling out to someone absent while believing that God creates the hearing in him.

The Wahhabis have shown ignorance in saying, at this juncture of the argument, that Islamic Law judges on the basis of externals *(al-hukm bi al-zahir)*, and that the external sense of calling upon someone other than God is that the caller believes in that other as having all-encompassing knowledge of the unseen and possessing an effective power to accomplish needs and complete disposal over the universe! Yet, they say, complete knowledge of the unseen and effective power to accomplish the needs of creatures are characteristics peculiar to the Creator: therefore, they conclude, belief that someone other than God is characterized in this way automatically constitutes ascribing a partner to God and disbelief.

---

[74]I.e. a Muslim.

The answer is that the external interpretation of the frame of mind of a person who supplicates someone other than God signifies only that the caller has called other than God. It does not signify that he believes that the one he calls has power to carry out one's needs nor any of the other attributes the Wahhabis mention.

Belief is an inward matter of which certain external phenomena might give indications. The act of calling is not one of them. Say to the Wahhabis who deem the external meaning of calling to be an indication of idolatry and disbelief: Why is it most of you don't consider what belongs to the Muslim whom you call a disbeliever from the side of his external behavior manifest in acts of prayer, fasting, zakat, and the other pillars of the Faith? Why do you not look at these as indicators of his faith and sound belief? What is more amazing, that same Muslim who engages in supplication, clearly articulates (by keeping the pillars) his disbelief in the own power of the one he calls to and in anything that goes with it. Yet despite this, you use this single external act of his as an indicator of that very belief which he has denied of himself. Would that I knew by what legal rule you can prove from the external significance of a man's call *(nida')* that his belief is deviant in the face of all the clear indications he gives you that his belief is sound.[75]

---

[75]From Abu Hurayra: I heard the Prophet (s) say: "By the one in Whose hand is Abu al-Qasim's soul, `Isa ibn Maryam shall descend as a just and wise ruler. He shall destroy the cross, slay the swine, eradicate discord and grudges, and money shall be offered to him but he will not accept it. Then he shall stand at my graveside and say: *Ya Muhammad!* and I will answer him."

Abu Ya`la relates it with a sound chain in his *Musnad* (Dar al-Ma'mun ed. 1407/1987) 11:462; Ibn Hajar cites it in *al-matalib al-`aliya* (Kuwait, 1393/1973) 4:23, chapter entitled: "The Prophet's life in his grave" and #4574; Haythami says in *Majma` al-zawa'id* (8:5), chapter entitled: "`Isa ibn Maryam's Descent": "Its sub-narrators are the men of sound (sahih) hadith."

Bukhari in his *Adab al-mufrad*, Nawawi in his *Adhkar*, and Shawkani in *Tuhfat al-dhakirin* all relate the narrations of Ibn `Umar and Ibn `Abbas whereby they would call out *Ya Muhammad* whenever

11: Wahhabis Claim: Anyone Visiting a Grave is a Disbeliever

Should one inquire as to the nature of Wahhabi doctrine and be curious as to what its objective is, the answer to both questions is easily summed up. It is their declaring all Muslims unbelievers. This answer is a sufficient definition of their entire school of thought. For the one who looks closely into the ideas they introduce will find that in each question that school strives to declare all Muslims unbelievers, even though God Himself is pleased with Islam as their religion:

- they have declared Muslims unbelievers for their assertion that God the Exalted transcends corporeality;
- they have declared Muslims unbelievers for their acceptance of Consensus is unbelief;
- they have declared Muslims unbelievers for their unquestioning emulation *(taqlid)* of the legal rulings concerning the faith made by the Imams, the mujtahids of the four schools of Islamic law;

---

they had a cramp in their leg (Chapters entitled: "What one says if he feels a cramp in his leg"). Regardless of the grade of these narrations, it is significant that Bukhari, Nawawi, and Shawkani never raised such a disturbing notion as to say that calling out "O Muhammad" amounted to shirk. See the following editions:

Nawawi's *Adhkar*:
1970 Riyadh edition: p. 271
1988 Ta'if edition: p. 383
1992 Mecca edition: p. 370

Bukhari's *Adab al-mufrad*:
1990 `Abd al-Baqi Beirut edition: p. 286
1994 Albani edition entitled *Da`if al-adab al-mufrad*: p. 87
The latter gives as a reference: *Takhrij al-kalim al-tayyib* (235)"
date? Beirut: `Alam al-kitab: p. 324
date? Beirut: Dar al-kutub al-`ilmiyya: p.142.

Shawkani's *Tuhfat al-dhakirin*:
1970 Beirut: Dar al-kutub al-`ilmiyya: p. 206-207.

- they have declared Muslims unbelievers for their seeking the Prophet's intercession *(istishfa`)* after his death and using him as a means to God *(tawassul)*;
- they have declared Muslims unbelievers for their visitation of graves.

To anyone who has eyes to see, it is obvious that a visitor to a grave either aims at seeking intercession, using as means to God those buried there and seeking to be blessed by visiting them, as in the case of visitation of places where prophets and saints are buried; or, on the other hand, the purpose may be consideration of the departed folk in order to strengthen feelings of humility in the heart and attain reward by reading the opening chapter of the Qur'an and asking God to forgive them, as when one visits the graves of all Muslims. Or, yet again, the aim of visitation may be remembrance of relatives and the departed beloved and visiting those whom fate has snatched away, of early making their graves their abodes. He remembers that they left him never to return again, feeling grief at their leave, his mind's tongue moving to express itself in lines like the following:

> O thou departing hence in pomp and power,
> Tarry a while, for thy ransom is pomp and power.
> Do not make haste, but walk humbly,
> For thou art leaving never to return again.

His sensibilities impel him to visit their graves, pausing at the traces of their tombs to shed sad tears over their remains and express their sorrow in lines like the following:

> Gone are those dear to me! and I remain, like a lone sword.
> How many a brother dearly beloved
> I laid in his grave by my own hand!

There is not in any of these practices one thing which calls for labeling as an unbeliever a Muslim bearing witness that there is no god but God and Muhammad is the Messenger of God. I do not think that even the uneducated and gullible among people, not to mention the learned person versed in Islamic Law, is ever so impelled by his ignorance as to intend, by his visitation of a grave, to worship it; nor that he would ever believe that the grave itself accomplishes his need and creates what he wants.

The Prophet's Order to Visit Graves The Prophet said: "I forbade you in the past to visit graves, but visit them. (For visiting graves promotes renunciation of this World and remembrance of the Hereafter)."[76] As for travels to visit graves, the ulama have had different opinions about it. Some of them make it illicit *(haram)* giving as evidence the words of the Prophet: "Do not travel except to three mosques: the Masjid al-Haram, this Masjid here in Madina, and Masjid al-Aqsa (in Jerusalem)." This is related by Bukhari, Muslim and al-Tirmidhi. Al-Qadi Husayn al-Marwazi (d. 462H) and al-Qadi `Iyad (d. 544H) have opted to forbid travel for visitation to graves[77] while others have permitted it, among them Imam al-Haramayn al-Juwayni and others. The proof they adduce for its permissibility is the Prophet's statement: "I have forbidden you in the past to visit graves, but visit them." They said the Prophet has commanded us in this hadith to visit graves, and that he did not differentiate between graves that are near and graves that are far and to visit which travel becomes necessary.

As for the hadith: "Do not travel except to three mosques..." he only forbade frequency of travel to mosques not to places of religious visitation, just as is clear from his words. He only forbade frequency of travel to mosques because one mosque is like the other and no city is devoid of a mosque; so there is no need for a journey. This is not the case with graves that are places of

---

[76]Muslim (Jana'iz, penultimate chapter; Adahi 37); Abu Dawud (Jana'iz 77; Ashriba 7); Tirmidhi (Jana'iz 7, 60); Nisa'i (Jana'iz 100; Dahaya 39; Ashriba 40); Ibn Majah (Jana'iz 47); Ahmad (1:145, 452; 3:38, 63, 66, 237, 250; 5:350, 355-357, 359, 361).

[77]This prohibition does not include the grave of the Prophet, concerning which visit `Iyad and Marwazi hold the same position as the *ijma`*, namely that it is a Sunna mustahabba.

visitation. They are not equal in blessing just as the hierarchical standing of their inhabitants differs in the view of God.

Without doubt, the exception expressed: "...except for three mosques" has several ramifications. Its meaning may be either the remote genus as when one says: "Do not travel anywhere except to three mosques." According to this meaning it is prohibited to travel anywhere other than what is expressed in the exception: this means that travel is illicit even for jihad, trading and commerce, gaining livelihood, acquiring knowledge and for pleasure and so forth. This cannot be the case. As for the proximate genus the meaning is: do not undertake travel to any mosque except to three. This is the correct interpretation. The hadith is specific in forbidding travel to all mosques except three. Thus, it is evidence for the permissibility for travel to visit graves.

`Umar, may God be pleased with him, after the conquest of Damascus said to Ka`b al-Ahbar: "O Ka`b, do you wish to come with us to Madina to visit the Messenger of God?" Ka`b answered: "Yes, O Commander of the Faithful." Similarly, we have evidence of Bilal's coming from Damascus to Madina to visit the grave of the Prophet. This took place during the caliphate of `Umar.[78]

Among those who say that traveling to visit graves is permissible we find Imam al-Nawawi, al-Qastallani, and Imam al-Ghazali. The latter said in his *Ihya' `Ulum al-Din* after mentioning the hadith: "Do not travel...": "The gist of the matter is that some ulama use it as evidence for prohibiting travel to places of religious visitation and pilgrimage. It is clear to me that this is not the case. On the contrary, visitation to graves is commanded by the hadith: "I have forbidden you in the past to visit graves, but visit them." The hadith only mentions the prohibition of visitation to other mosques than the three Mosques because of the likeness of one mosque to another. Furthermore, there is no city in which there is no mosque.

---

[78]Shawkani in *Nayl al-awtar* confirms that Bilal undertook travel for the express purpose of visiting the Prophet (s) according to a report with a good chain in hafiz Ibn `Asakir's *Tarikh Dimashq*.

Hence, there is no need to travel to another mosque. As for places of religious visitation, the *baraka* of visiting them varies to the measure of their rank with God."

Touching on the issue of whether dead people hear or not, our view is as follows. It is well known that hearing in living people is actually a property of spirit *(al-Ruh)*. The ear is only an organ or rather instrument of hearing, nothing more. Since the spirit of the dead person does not become extinct with the extinction of his body, the belief that the spirit hears is not farfetched. One cannot claim that it does not hear due to loss of the organ of hearing by reason of the body's perishing. For we say that it sometimes hears even without that organ just as in visions. Thus, the spirit talks and hears in its sleep just as it sees in dreams without mediation of an instrument, that is, an organ of sensation. Then, is it too much for the rational person, after experiencing sound and sight in one's sleep by the sole means of the spirit and without the slightest participation of the organs of sound and sight, to believe that after the spirit separates from the body it hears and sees even without the organs of sound and sight?

Yet and still, the Wahhabis do not extend their denial that the dead can hear to martyrs because God says: "Do not consider those who are slain for God's sake dead, but they are alive receiving sustenance with their Lord" (3:169). There is no doubt that the rank of prophets is not beneath the rank of martyrs: they, like them, are alive with their Lord, receiving sustenance. It has been narrated that the Prophet said: "I passed by Musa on the night of my Journey while he was praying in his grave."[79] And on the authority of Anas the Prophet said: "Prophets are alive in their graves [praying]."[80]

---

[79]A sound (sahih) tradition related on the authority of Anas and others by Muslim, Nasa'i, Bayhaqi in the *Dala'il al-nubuwwa* and the *Hayat al-anbiya*, and Suyuti in *Anba' al-adhkya'* and *Sharh al-sudur*. Nawawi said in his commentary on this hadith: "The work of the next world is all dhikr and du`a" (*Sharh Sahih Muslim* 1/73/267).

[80]A sound (sahih) tradition related on the authority of Anas ibn Malik (r) by al-Bazzar in his *Musnad*, Abu Ya`la in his *Musnad*, Ibn `Adi in *al-Kamil fi al-du`afa'*, Tammam al-Razi in *al-Fawa'id*, al-

Abu Ya`la al-Mawsili and al-Bazzar relate this. On the authority of Ibn `Umar the Prophet said: "I saw Jesus, Moses, and Abraham, on them be peace." This is related by Bukhari, Muslim and Imam Malik in his *Muwatta'*. Al-Bayhaqi recorded in *Shu`ab al-Iman* on the authority of Abu Hurayra that the Prophet said: "Whoever sends blessings on me at my grave, I will hear him, and whoever sends blessings on me from afar, I am informed about it."[81] Therefore, if the premise *prophets are alive* is affirmed, one must also affirm the premise *prophets can hear*; for hearing is a concomitant property of life. It is incorrect to claim that since the life of prophets and martyrs in the *barzakh* is different from the life of this world they cannot hear. Even if we grant that the two lives differ in kind, nevertheless affirming "They are alive" with *any* kind of life is sufficient to establish that they hear and that their tawassul and supplication for help follows as a matter of course.

Bayhaqi in *Hayat al-anbiya' fi quburihim*, Abu Nu`aym in *Akhbar Asbahan*, Ibn `Asakir in *Tarikh Dimashq*, al-Haythami in *Majma` al-zawa'id* (8:211), al-Suyuti in *Anba' al-adhkiya' bi-hayat al-anbiya'* (#5), and al-Albani, in *Silsilat al-ahadith al-sahihah* (#621). Suyuti adds: "The life of the Prophet, may Allah bless him and give him peace, in his grave, and [also] that of the rest of the prophets is known to us as definitive knowledge *(`ilman qat`iyyan)*." Sakhawi, Ibn Hajar al-`Asqalani's student, said: "As for us (Muslims) we believe and we confirm that he (s) is alive and provided for *in his grave*" (*al-Qawl al-badi`* p. 161). Ibn al-Qayyim said in *Kitab al-Ruh* p. 58: "It is obligatory knowledge to know that his body (s) is in the earth tender and humid (i.e. as in life), and when the Companions asked him: 'How is our greeting presented to you after you have turned to dust' he replied: 'God has defended the earth from consuming the flesh of Prophets,' and if his body were not in his grave he would not have given this answer."

[81] Abu al-Shaykh cites it in *Kitab al-Salat `ala al-nabi* ("*Jala' al-afham*" p. 22), and Ibn Hajar says in *Fath al-Bari* (6:379): "Abu al-Shaykh cites it with a good chain *(sanad jayyid)*." Bayhaqi mentions it in *Hayat al-anbiya* and *Shu`ab al-iman* (2:218 #1583). The hadith suggests that there is no difference whatsoever in the hearing of the Prophet whether greeted from near or far. He hears *as-salamu `alayka ya rasul Allah* equally whether the person greeting him is in Madina or in America. Utter respect in manner and bearing is due in either case, such as standing with awe and reverence.

Finally, the organ of hearing itself, in prophets, is not voided by death: for their bodies do not suffer the corruption of the grave as we know from the noble hadith: "God has forbidden the earth to consume the bodies of Prophets."[82] If we were to slacken the reins and say it is true that the bodies of prophets undergo corruption in their graves as the Wahhabis claim, having already affirmed that *they are alive and receiving sustenance* (3:169), then, this would simply count as affirmation that they hear even though they lack an organ for this purpose according to the view we expounded above.

We have abundant evidence in hadith which provide evidence that other than prophets and martyrs among the dead can hear. Cited by Bukhari and Muslim and the narrators of the *Sunan* is the hadith transmitted on the authority of Ibn `Umar who said: "The Messenger of God spoke to the People (buried) in the Well saying: "Have you found out that what your Lord had promised you is true?" then someone exclaimed: "Are you calling out to the dead!" The Prophet replied: "You do not hear better than they do, except they do not respond."" And in Bukhari and Muslim we find the hadith of Anas on the authority of Abu Talha that the Prophet called to them: "O Abu Jahl Ibn Hisham! O Umayya Ibn Khalaf! O `Utba ibn Rabi`a! Have you not found out that what your Lord promised you is true? for I have found that what he has promised me is true." `Umar said to him: "O Messenger of God, how do you address bodies devoid of spirit?" The Prophet replied: "By Him Who holds my life in His Hands! You do not hear what I am saying to them better than they do." Similarly, it has been affirmed in

---

[82] A sound (sahih) tradition related on the authority of Aws ibn Aws al-Thaqafi by: Ahmad in his *Musnad*, Ibn Abi Shaybah in the *Musannaf*, Abu Dawud in the *Sunan*, Nisa'i in his *Sunan*, Ibn Majah in his *Sunan*, Darimi in his *Musnad*, Ibn Khuzaymah in his *Sahih*, Ibn Hibban in his *Sahih*, Hakim in the *Mustadrak*, Tabarani in his *Kabir*, Bayhaqi in *Hayat al-anbiya'*, Suyuti in *Anba' al-adkhiya*, Dhahabi who confirmed al-Hakim's grading, and Nawawi in the *Adhkar*. Another version in Ibn Majah has this addition: "And the Prophet of Allah is alive and provided for *(fa nabiyyullahi hayyun yurzaq)*." Bayhaqi mentions it also in the *Sunan al-kubra*.

Bukhari and Muslim on the authority of Anas that the Prophet said: "Surely, when the servant of God is placed in his grave and his companions in this life turn away from it, he hears the thumps of their sandaled feet."[83]

Abu Nu`aym Al-Isbahani has mentioned with his chain of transmission from `Ubayd Ibn Marzuq who said: "A woman of Madina, named Umm Mihjan, used to sweep the mosque, then she died. The Prophet was not told of this event. Thereafter, he passed over her grave and queried: "What is this?" Those present replied: "Umm Mihjan." He said: "The one who swept the mosque?" They answered: "Yes." Thereupon the people lined up and prayed for her. Then he addressed her: "Which work of yours did you find more favored?" They exclaimed: "O Messenger of God, can she hear you?" He replied: "You cannot hear better than she does." Then it is mentioned that she answered him: "Sweeping the mosque." The chain of transmission in this hadith is interrupted. There are others more like it.[84]

It is narrated concerning `A'isha, may God be pleased with her, when she heard the hadith about the dead hearing, she denied it and said: "How does the Prophet say something like that when God has said: "You cannot make those to hear who are in the graves" (35:22). While her opinion does not affirm the hearing of the dead as Ibn Taymiyya notes in his Legal Opinions *(Fatawa)* and in other places, we have no excuse for following it. For the question necessarily concerns a well-known matter of faith which no one has permission to deny. In fact `A'isha has also narrated that the Prophet said, as Ibn Rajab has noted in *Ahwal al-Qubur*: "Surely they know now that what I said to them is true." This narration of

---

[83]See also the "Chapter on the Proofs Used to Establish the Knowledge that the Dead Hear in the Graves" in Ibn al-Qayyim's *al-Ruh* and similar chapters in Suyuti's *Sharh al-sudur*, Ibn al-Kharrat's *al-`Aqiba*, Ibn Rajab's *Ahwal al-qubur*, Subki's *Shifa' al-siqam* and others.

[84]Ibn Hajar says in *al-Isaba* (8:187): "Mihjana, also named Umm Mihjan: a black woman who used to sweep the mosque [in Madina]. She is mentioned in the books of sound (sahih) hadith but without being named."

hers supports those which say that the dead hear, for if it is possible for a dead man to know, surely it is possible for him also to hear. Therefore, to affirm that they do know is necessarily also to affirm that they hear.

As for the Qur'anic verses: "You cannot make those who are in the graves hear" (35:22) and: "You cannot make the dead hear..." (27:80) there is no evidence in them for the denial of hearing in the case of the dead in the absolute sense, it is only evidence for denying hearing for those who benefit thereof.[85] That is because what is meant by the phrase: "Those in the graves" in the first verse and by "the dead" in the second verse are the unbelievers, who are compared to the dead lying in their graves. Just as the dead do not hear with a beneficial kind of hearing -- that is, with a hearing made complete by the mutual exchange of address between the hearer and the speaker -- in the same way the unbelievers do not hear the warning signs that the Prophet addresses to them in a way that benefits them by guiding them to faith in God.

What otherwise confirms the above is that unqualified hearing is also an established attribute of the unbelievers: they hear what the Prophet said to them; but they derived no benefit from it. This is confirmed by God's saying: "If God had recognized in them any good, He would, indeed, have made them hear: if He made them hear (as it stands), they would turn away" (8:23). Hence, what is meant by "hear" when He says "He would indeed have made them hear" is a hearing which brings benefit to the hearer and when He says: "If He made them hear (as it stands)" He means hearing which carries no benefit. If this were otherwise, the sense of the passage would be corrupt inasmuch as the verse would, then, be a syllogism where the middle term (He makes them hear) is

---

[85]See Ibn Qayyim's section "That the Hearing of the Dead is Real" in *Al-Ruh* (Madani ed. 1984) p. 59: "The actual meaning of these verses (35:22 and 27:80) is: You cannot make those hear whom God does not wish to hear, for you are only a Warner. That is: God has only given you the ability to warn, for which he has made you responsible; not that of making those to hear whom God does not wish to hear."

reiterated; the end result would be: "If God had recognized any good in them, they would have turned away." This conclusion is absurd and contradictory, as you can see, since it would entail that the turning back take place -- which is evil -- despite the fact that God recognized good in them. God's recognition would be, in that case, a misrecognition with respect to the true state of the unbelievers -- Exalted is God high above such a possibility.

The above cited two verses point to a further meaning: that what is meant by the hearing negated in both cases is the hearing connected with the faculty of guidance just as the context of the two verses indicate. The meaning then is that you do not guide the unbelievers by yourself, O Muhammad! because they are like dead men and that you cannot cause the dead to hear by yourself. The only agent causing them to hear is God as the Qur'an says: "You do not guide whom you like but God guides whom he wishes" (28:56).

One does not say: "Just as the one making the dead to hear in reality is God, likewise, the one making the living to hear is in reality none other than He." For God is the Creator of all actions whatsoever, just as the true doctrine on the matter teaches. What, then, is the motivation for illustrating God's agency with the hearing of the dead? What we say is this:

1- The fact that God alone is the one making the dead to hear is a matter admitting of no ambiguity even for a blind man. As for His being the one causing the living to hear in reality, it is not said like that.[86] This is because one might falsely suppose that the Agent causing hearing in the one spoken to is the actual speaker, on the grounds that the hearing of the one spoken to directly follows the external voice issuing from the mouth of the person who addresses him. Hence to exemplify God's agency with the hearing of the living is improper. To give an example requires that its content be unambiguously clear; this

[86] I.e. it is inappropriate to use such terms.

is not the case in the category of living persons as we have explained.[87]

2- Since the unbelievers were alive, to illustrate the fact that the Prophet cannot make them hear by comparing them to the living whom the Prophet cannot cause to hear comes close to fashioning a comparison between a thing and itself, as we find in that given by the poet who said:

> Surrounded as we are with water,
> We sit like people encircled by water.

The Wahhabis respond, with regard to the hadith of the People of the Well, that the hearing experienced by the dead on the occasion when the Prophet questioned them was a miracle proper only to him. It does not count as evidence, they claim, that these dead were also capable of hearing the speech of someone else. The answer to this is that the miracle is not a miracle unless its manifestation is a phenomenon experienced by other persons like the speaking of pebbles. The Companions were hearing the voice of the pebbles glorifying God while they were being held in the palm of the Prophet's hand.[88] But it is impossible that the dead's hearing of the Prophet speaking to them be a miracle since it was not manifest to anyone but himself. Furthermore, the hadith reporting that the dead hear the thumping of sandaled feet (Bukhari and Muslim) contravenes such a phenomenon being a miracle in the case of the People of the Well. For it indicates that dead people also hear the talk of other people besides the Prophet.

---

[87]Zahawi's point is that God highlighted the power to make the dead hear in the Qur'an as an example of His agency, because in the case of the dead, His agency is more evident to the mind than in the case of the living, although He equally effects the hearing of both the living and the dead.

[88]Hadith of Abu Dharr related by Haythami in "Majma` al-zawa'id" with a sound (sahih) chain, chapter entitled *`Alamat al-nubuwwa* (Signs of Prophethood): "The Prophet took pebbles and they glorified God in his hand; he put them down and they became silent..."

The Wahhabis further respond that the object intended when the Prophet spoke to the dead was admonition of the living and not to cause an act of understanding on the part of the dead. The answer to this is that if the intended object of his speech was admonition of the living, why did `Umar ask: "How do you speak to bodies devoid of spirit?" out of astonishment at his speaking to them? I do not believe that fatuousness has pushed the Wahhabis to the point of thinking that after almost three-quarters of a millennium they understand what the Prophet meant better than his Companion, `Umar. Besides, the answer the Prophet gave by itself constitutes denial that what he aimed at was admonition because he replied: "You do not hear better than they." This answer is obviously not suitable as an admonition. On the contrary, it is a clear rejection of `Umar's sense of farfetchedness in the Prophet's behavior and astonishment because of it.

The Wahhabis, finally, answer that the Prophet only spoke to the dead out of personal conviction that they hear. Thereafter, they claim, the two verses of the Qur'an were revealed to correct his belief. The response to this is that it is unallowable that the Prophet believed anything like that of his own accord. On the contrary, it came about necessarily in virtue of revelation and inspiration from his Lord. God said of him: "He does not speak of his own desire" (53:3). This is especially the case since he did not arrive at his knowledge of the matter by merely exercising his faculty of reason. Rather, it came about by way of revelation and inspiration as we have said.

One piece of evidence that indicates that God quickens the dead in their graves so that they hear is His statement retelling the avowal of those who said: "Our Lord, twice hast Thou put us to death and twice hast Thou quickened us" (40:11). For what is meant by the first putting to death is the putting to death before resting in the grave. What is meant in the case of the other is the putting to death after resting in the grave. If God did not give life in the graves a second time, it would be impossible to put to death a second time. The Wahhabis answer this by saying that the first putting to death is the state of nonexistence prior to creation and the second putting to death is after creation. In truth, this is amusing even for children because putting to death can take place only after the occurrence of life and there is no life prior to God's creation of life. As for their response that the first putting to death is the putting to death of people after their life in the world of atoms, it is weaker than the first answer. People in the world of atoms were no different than spirits which God created and asked: "Am I not your Lord? and they answered, saying: Yes!" (7:172). Moreover, the reader knows that death is defined as a separation of the soul from the body. Hence, there is no death prior to embodiment, although it is possible for God to annihilate spirits after creating them. But that has nothing to do with death as we have just defined it.

Finally, the Wahhabiyya usher forth evidence for the incapacity of dead people to hear on the basis of a legal ruling of the Shari`a that ulama apply in the case where a man performs certain acts using such words as: "If I address X, my wife is divorced" -- or: "my slave-girl is free." Now, if that man speaks to X after his death, then the divorce is invalid and the act of manumission null. They conclude that the basis of nullity and voidness is the fact that dead person lacks the faculty of hearing.

We refuse to grant that the basis of the ruling for the ulama is the absence of hearing on the part of the dead. On the contrary, they base themselves on what they know of custom, namely that it routinely makes the stipulating of oaths like the above, conditional on life. The whole benefit of speaking is the mutual exchange of communication, which does not place when one party of the communication is dead. Conversing with a dead person, therefore, does not qualify as speech only inasmuch as his death renders him powerless to respond -- not because he is powerless to hear.

12: The Wahhabis' *takfir* of the one who swears, makes a vow, or sacrifices by other than God

May God the Exalted fight the Wahhabis because they are intent on establishing reasons to declare Muslims unbelievers. They have shown that *takfir* is their highest ambition.

You see them declaring as disbelievers persons who implore God for the sake of the Prophet and seek his help by intercession to God to accomplish their needs, while not feeling the slightest shame in seeking help from unbelievers of the foreign states of Europe[89] in order to carry out their plans which are to subject the Muslims to their control, make war against them, and, in rebellion from the authority of the Commander of the Faithful, renounce allegiance to him and the obedience to him which God has ordered in the Qur'an as we have explained earlier. They have taken the enemies of Islam as intimate friends, asking them to aid them with military support in their corrupt purpose and using that support to perpetrate their stubborn harassment and error. Yet God has said: "O ye who believe! take not the Jews and the Christians for your friends and protectors" (5:54). May our Lord remove the Wahhabis from the face of the earth. Do they not know that those same "friends" they make in order to subjugate Muslims to their tyranny, will, once they have gotten a foothold, in turn, subjugate and oppress them as well along with whomever else they consider adverse and opposed to their plans?

We have shown that the practice of the Wahhabis is to declare all Muslims disbelievers. As we already said, they claim they are unbelievers because they implore God for the sake of prophets and saints and, in addition, call on them for help. Wahhabis also claim that Muslims are unbelievers if they swear by the name of someone else than God and make vows to other than Him and sacrifice animals for their sake.

For the sake of argument, let us grant that certain doctrines which the Wahhabis attribute to Muslims are held by them and do in fact constitute disbelief, and that it is correct to say that the person asserting them has acted contrary to Islam. Even then, it would still not be correct to pronounce the entire community of Muslims guilty of unbelief or even a specific Muslim individual. For the latter might have made such a statement lacking knowledge of whatever texts would obligate acknowledgment of the truth. Or

---

[89] And now America.

it might be the case that such knowledge has not been suitably established in his view. Or perhaps he has not understood it and had what confuses him laid out in a fashion that allows him to beg forgiveness before God and seek proper excuses for his error. For the one who believes in God and His Messenger, God is a Forgiver of sins whether committed in thought, word, or deed. As for the more severe aspect of what He has revealed in the Qur'an concerning those who perpetrates those sins, it comes in the form of threats and, as it says, is meant for: "Whoever kills a believer intentionally, his recompense is Hell to abide therein" (4:93); and "Those who unjustly eat up the property of orphans, eat a fire into their own bodies: they will soon be enduring a blazing fire" (4:10); and: "Those who disobey God and His Messenger and transgress His limits will be admitted to a Fire, to abide therein: and they shall have a humiliating punishment" (4:14).

In his book *Madarij al-salikin*, Ibn al-Qayyim has made the statement, the gist of which is as follows: The adherents of the Sunna of the Prophet are in complete agreement that God's friendship and enmity might be found in the single individual in two different respects: there might exist in him faith and hypocrisy, as well as faith and unbelief together. In addition, he will be close to God in one respect more than the other. Hence, of the people in one respect the Qur'an says: "They were that day nearer to unbelief than to faith" (3:167). Associating a partner with God -- *shirk* -- falls into two classes: hidden and manifest. Hidden shirk might be forgiven. As for manifest shirk, there is no forgiveness for it without express repentance.

Now swearing by someone other than God -- Ibn Qayyim continues -- does not remove the one who does it from Islam, even though there is mentioned in a hadith narrated on the authority of Ibn `Umar that: "Whoever swears by someone other than God has associated a partner with Him."[90] And in another narration of the same hadith: "Whoever swears by someone other than God has

---

[90]A sound (sahih) hadith related by Abu Dawud, Iman 3:570 (3251), and Tirmidhi, Iman 5:253 (1535).

committed an act of *kufr*." The leading scholars of hadith in the schools of Shafi`i, Hanafi, Maliki and Hanbali law all construe *kufr* here to mean *kufr al-ni`ma* or the failure to acknowledge God's favor or blessing. As for the shirk mentioned in the first narration, they find it to be *al-shirk al-khafi* or the kind that is hidden rather than manifest such as occurs when one performs an act of piety in order to show off. That does not remove a person from Islam. Yet it defeats the religious purpose of that act. On this much the ulama have reached a consensus so that those who follow the school of Imam Shafi`i, for example, say that it falls into the category of what is *makruh tanzihan* or reprehensible for purposes of scrupulous observance, rather than *makruh tahriman* or reprehensible to the point of prohibition and reprobation. Therefore, the mode of swearing about which the ulama disagree over whether it is reprehensible or prohibited cannot be said to make its perpetrator an unbeliever and thus remove him from Islam.[91]

As for the vow to someone other than God, both Shaykh Taqi al-Din Ibn Taymiyya and Ibn al-Qayyim -- who are among the most critical concerning this question -- said that it is not

---

[91]This is Ibn Qayyim's text in *Kitab al-Salat* of the *Madarij*: "About Greater Shirk Allah says: "Surely whoever ascribes partners to Allah, for him Allah has forbidden the Garden. His abode is the Fire. For wrong-doers there will be no helpers" (5:72); and also: "Whoever ascribes partners to Allah, it is as if he had fallen from the sky and the birds had snatched him or the wind blown him to a far-off place" (22:31). About showing off He says: "And whoever hopes for the meeting with his Lord, let him do righteous works, and associate no partner in the worship due only to his Lord" (18:110).

"On this same subject of Lesser Shirk, the Prophet, may Allah bless him and grant him peace, said: "Whoever swears an oath by other than Allah has associated something with Him." This was related by Abu Dawud and others. However, it is well known that swearing an oath by something other than Allah does not take one out of the community of the Muslims, and it does not make someone a disbeliever. In the same vein the Prophet said: "*Shirk* in this Umma is stealthier than creeping ants." [Ahmad 4:403; Albani considers it sound in *Sahih al-Jami` al-saghir*, 3:333 (3624).]

permissible and that it constitutes an act of disobedience. Neither said that it constitutes an act of unbelief or of *shirk* such as would remove one from Islam. Their position is that fulfilling such a vow is not allowable, but that if the vow is to give alms to some deserving person among the poor, then, it is good for him in the sight of God. Now, if the one making the vow to someone other than God were an unbeliever then they would not have ordered him to perform an act of charity since charity is unacceptable from an unbeliever. Rather, they would have ordered him to renew his Islam.

As for the sacrifice for the sake of someone other than God, Ibn Qayyim categorizes it under things prohibited, not under act of unbelief, except when one sacrifices to something worshipped besides the Creator. Similarly, those versed in knowledge record that it is prohibited because it is for the sake of someone other than God. Nevertheless, they do not declare the one who performs such a sacrifice an unbeliever.

Conclusion What I intended to elaborate in this hastily thrown together work has now been accomplished. My purpose has been to prevent the spread of the Wahhabi school into Iraq and neighboring areas, to clarify for the individual reader the truth, and unveil for him what is correct. He should no longer be deceived by whatever this subversive sect publishes to infect with its views the ignorant and the simple-minded.

My efforts in this work have been aided by my brother and friend in Islam, the learned Ma`ruf Effendi al-Risafi, may the Creator long sustain him. And praise belongs to God first and last.

The indigent one relying on God the Exalted
Jamil Effendi Zahawi Zadah
Beginning of Ramadan 1322 A.H. (1904 C.E.)

INDEX OF QUR'ANIC VERSES

INDEX OF HADITHS AND REPORTS